The Digital Delusion

How to Overcome the Misguidance and Misinformation Online

7 Simple Steps to Becoming The Online Leader In Your Industry

by Doyle Buehler

THE DIGITAL DELUSION

How To Overcome The Misguidance and Misinformation Online To Become The Leader In Your Industry

First published in Australia in 2014 by

The Digital Delusion

Visit our website at: www.thedigitaldelusion.com

Email: doyle@thedigitaldelusion.com

© Doyle Robert Buehler 2014

All rights reserved. No part of this publication may be reproduced, stored in a retrieval system, or transmitted in any form or by any means, electronic, mechanical, photocopying, recording or otherwise, without the prior written permission of the author or publisher.

National Library of Australia Cataloguing-in-Publication entry

Author:	Buehler, Doyle Robert, 1969-
Title:	The Digital Delusion: How To Overcome The Misguidance and Misinformation Online To Become The Leader In Your Industry
ISBN:	978-0-9874990-0-4　(Ppbk – The Digital Delusion)
	978-0-9874990-1-1　(PDF – The Digital Delusion)
	978-0-9874990-2-8　(ePub – The Digital Delusion)
	978-0-9874990-3-5　(mobi – The Digital Delusion)
Notes:	Bibliography, includes Index
Subjects:	Buehler, Doyle
	Internet Marketing
	Social Media
	Web sites – Design
	Content Marketing
	Business Strategy
Dewey Number:	658.872

Author Photo by Ben Scott
Cover Design by Sweetlips Design
Edited by Ann Sumich

WORDS OF PRAISE FOR THE DIGITAL DELUSION

"Buehler invites us along as he travels up the various digital tributaries into the mystical heart of darkness that is the digital industry, where we encounter the monkey and reptilian tribes that inhabit these parts and the digital extremists, false gurus and the downright rogues that lead them. He then systematically asks us to recognise the self-perpetuating fraud that is the norm here and brings some real light into the otherwise heated, cluttered and confusing world of online. It was well worth the trip."

John Lynch
Entrepreneur
Climbing Fish Ltd, Digital Ministry

"Most entrepreneurs still have their heads in the sand when it comes to their online strategy and Doyle pulls no punches with this book as he offers a proven methodology for driving serious results online."

Glen Carlson
CEO
Key Person Of Influence Australia

"Let online expert Doyle Buehler be your coach and guide through the world of digital marketing. Practical, down to earth, and full of "how-to" advice, this book will help you become the leader in your field or industry."

Matthew Michalewicz
Author of Life in a Half Second
www.Michalewicz.com.au

"At long last the Digital Delusion is smashed. There is so much misinformation and downright confusion about the online world, thank goodness someone has finally written the book to make sense of it all. Doyle Buehler gives all the right information, delivered in a no BS way, that is the key to actually making the most of the online world and social media in any business."

Andrew Griffith
Australia's #1 Small Business and Entrepreneurial Author.

The Digital Delusion

Doyle Buehler

"I have traveled the length and breadth of this country and talked with the best people, and I can assure you that data processing is a fad that won't last out the year."
- Prentice Hall editor in charge of business books, 1957

INCLUDES FREE ENTREPRENEURS ONLINE TRAINING COURSE

Get the exclusive Digital Strategy Training course for readers only. Over 20+ hours of content and $367 in value. Email thebook@thedigitaldelusion.com for complete course access now.

DOWNLOAD THE FREE PDF VERSION OF
THE DIGITAL DELUSION

Get a digital PDF copy for your smartphone, tablet or ebook reader. Email doyle@thedigitaldelusion.com to get your free copy now.

TABLE OF CONTENTS

Introduction xv

Chapter One: The Show Is About To Begin 1
    The Beginnings 2
    What You Need to Actually Read This Book 3
    Connecting & Sharing With This Book 4
    How To Get the Most from this book 5
    My Digital Journey So Far 9

Chapter Two: The Digital Delusion Manifesto 13
    State of the Affairs 14
    Empire Builders 18
    Are You The Master of Your Digital Domain? 25
    The Digital Delusion Manifesto 28

Chapter Three: The 7 Deadly Digital Delusions 33
    What You Need To Know 34
    The Digital Delusions 35
    Are You Delusional? The Mini-Audit 36
    What Defines a Delusion? 37
    What are the 7 Deadly Digital Delusions? 38
    Why We Are Delusional 40
    Deadly Digital Delusion #1 42
    Deadly Digital Delusion #2 47
    Deadly Digital Delusion #3 50
    Deadly Digital Delusion #4 53
    Deadly Digital Delusion #5 57
    Deadly Digital Delusion #6 60
    Deadly Digital Delusion #7 63
    Defeating the Digital Delusions 66

Chapter Four: Online Love & The Digital Detox 69
    What You Need To Know 70
    Getting to Therapy 71
    Online Customer Love 72
    The Digital Detox 76

Chapter Five: Digital Trends That Are Shaping Your Business & Key Elements of Online Success 81
    What You Need To Know 82
    Dominant Trends For Online Businesses 83
    Telling 86
    Connecting 88
    Editing 91
    The 3 Elements of Your Online Business – A Strategic Architecture for Digital Businesses 95
    The 17 Digital Components To Master Your Digital Domain 99
    Setting Online Goals 104

Chapter Six: The Online Empire Project 107
    What You Need To Know 108
    Introduction to the Online Empire Project 109
    What Is Empire Building Online About? 109
    Building Your Online Empire 111
    How to Become Awesome Online: The Basics of Building Your Online Business Breakthrough. 112
    Building Your Online Empire 113
    You Are Your Own Brand 114
    Frame By Frame - Building an Online Breakthrough For Your Business 115
    What You Need to Do to Engage in Building Your Empire Online 120
    How Does This Fit With Your Business? 120
    Frame 1: Strategy 121
    Frame 2: Content 124
    Frame 3: Social & Sharing 130

    Frame 4: Video & Visuals..133
        Part 1: Video...133
        Part 2: Visuals..136
    Frame 5: Website Alignment...139
    Frame 6: Sales Funnel & Goals...145
    Frame 7: Analytics, Advertising 149

Chapter Seven: Next Steps and Action Plan 153
    What You Need To Know 154
    The New Digital Manifesto..155
    Rules of ENGAGEment 155
    Other Resources..157
    Tools 157
    Online Empire Project - Resources 158
    Create A Master Schedule 158
    Your New Scorecard..160
    Your Free Entrepreneur Online Training Course....................... 161
    Education..162

Where to find us!... 165
Other Products & Services 167
Acknowledgments... 169
Crowdfunding & Supporters.. 170
References 172
Bibliography.. 173
About The Author... 175

INTRODUCTION

Many businesses are doing numerous things incorrectly online, yet expecting some miraculous moment where everything will suddenly be relevant. "Maybe that video of the cat that was posted last week will go "viral" or maybe those hilarious photos of the bacon that were posted last month will finally make a difference". This book is not about "maybes". This book is not about creating a new viral video that will spread like wildfire. Yes, Facebook is not the be all and end all, it is simply a tool that can be in your toolkit, or not.

This book is not just about how to use Facebook or other social media websites, how to be "The King of Content", or how to optimise for SEO, it is far more than that. The online world is full of so many "buzzwords" that simply have lost any significance what-so-ever to the actual core principles of running a business.

While some may love the word "guru" because it implies a certain level of knowledge and trust; there is an awful lot of "mistrust and misinformation" from so-called and often self-proclaimed gurus in the digital media industries. More often than not, these people are really only trying to demonstrate how much they know about the online world, in the hopes of making a sale to someone. There are far too many hi-costing programs that return very little in overall value or action. This has to stop. What is needed is a champion, not a guru, or an expert. Fundamentally, it is about knowing and understanding what is important to your business and your industry - no one can do that beside yourself. You need to be the leader in your industry. The ideas in this book will help you get there.

It is true that some businesses are "working it" and "working it well" online. If you are like the rest, you have probably wondered exactly how they are doing it right, or why it is actually working for them. The difference is? They have a system, a platform, and a framework; a framework that puts everything that they do into context and shows the relative importance of each aspect.

This book is for business leaders and entrepreneurs who are ready to move their business to the next level. It is about bringing on your A-game. There are no prizes for second place. This is for entrepreneurs, business-leaders, and forward thinkers who have the guts to get things done, and the heart to know that no one does it better than themselves.

Firstly, let's get it out of the way - being online is not easy.

There are so many challenges online that are really overwhelming. While some businesses simply give up, some attempts are futile in that nothing is achieved, and all to no avail. There are many frustrations that further exacerbate the difficulties online, one being the massive abundance of choice. Direct advertising has jaded many, and attention spans have become shorter than most goldfish. How do you stand out amongst all of this and actually grow, sustain and build a business under these conditions?

It is very confusing, even for someone like myself who has been involved directly in the industry for over a decade. What sometimes seemed like a mess of mass confusion, the deeper I searched, patterns started to appear. Patterns that seemed to be going nowhere; a different state of operations that just did not seem to work like they should have.

> "Are you an entrepreneur wanting to stand-out and be different online? So are 400 Million in 54 Countries around the world."
>
> (Global Entrepreneurship Monitor, 2011)

The status quo wasn't working –
businesses were still struggling to get sales, leads, and engagement. It wasn't a pretty picture at all. The problem was that businesses could not believe, nor understand, why things were not working properly online, or why they weren't working as well as they were told.

Many businesses did not actually realise what pieces were missing, and how critical it was to understand what they needed to do, how to do it, and when. Entrepreneurs were really feeling STUCK, overwhelmed, and even mislead.

The unfortunate aspect was that many entrepreneurs simply didn't know what they didn't know; they didn't have the knowledge to bridge that gap.

These were all part of what I then coined as The Digital Delusions, and they are very real.

This book is about identifying the underlying patterns or delusions that have been occurring with online businesses of all shapes and sizes. It is about taking these negative aspects, and working them into a structure and framework that then assists business leaders to work in a dynamic, systematic manner. It is about turning digital media on its head and making a difference.

This book deals with these delusions that are affecting how a business is built and advanced online. "But", you are saying, "isn't a delusion about some psychosis, or worse yet, some belief that things are better than they seem"? Of course, the answer is a resounding, yes. Yes, what has been learned and taught has simply lulled everyone into a false sense of security. A sense where everything seems just fine, and that everything will work out ok. Nothing could really be further from the truth.

> "What exactly is a Digital Delusion? How does it affect me?

The delusions presented are what are literally and figuratively slowing businesses down. They are getting in the way of what should be done, or worse yet, what you know should be occurring. The delusions are what businesses need to be doing differently in order to get to the business breakthrough and the success desired.

One thing needs to be made clear. Delusions are not "myths". This is not a list of myths about the online industry. Myths are like fables or fairy tales; delusions are what are behind the myths, as they are actually a way of thinking. Delusions are actual behaviours, not just a story.

More often than not, books of this nature are focused on advertising agencies, the marketer or the market researcher. The business leader and entrepreneur, however, are often missed. This book is for these leaders who can actually influence and implement strategies.

Since 2004, I have spent a number of years in the online, e-commerce worlds, including start-ups, media agencies and everything in between. I have developed many online systems, including developing online strategies, advertising campaigns, social media activities, community building, and everything else. I have seen what works and what doesn't work. I have seen what some companies truly understand, and where other companies are simply missing the point. What has been quite predominant is that the companies that are making online strategies "work" for them are the companies that are able to integrate all the different segments of an online strategy. They have been able to put the different pieces together, despite the seemingly varied nature of them. This is what this book is about - providing a clear segmentation of what is needed, and further creating a defining framework that allows the business leader to find their triumphs online.

This book is not a negative-take on everything that is wrong, either. While there are some aspects that are blatantly incorrect and misguided, these issues need to be brought to the forefront and businesses need to confront them, so that they can better understand them and make improvements on how to do things. It is not just about highlighting where businesses are being misled, importantly, it is about what can be done about it to get everything back on track.

Perhaps entrepreneurs believe that they will always be positive and optimistic, that there will always be customers, that people will always "like" their "stuff" online. Everyone wants success in their business, and, as online is still somewhat new, many are unsure of what to do. It is easy to get caught up in the buzzwords and "guru-speak" that further perpetuate the myths and delusions, without realising there is actually something bigger and better. "You just need to do this...", are the thoughts that many have.

Businesses have taken these so-called truths, and created a sense of malaise, and almost a sense of reservation, that things will get better, "if only I did....". And, so the tail chasing begins with nothing really working very well, or some things working with entrepreneurs having absolutely no idea why. Unfortunately, the worse scenario would be for nothing to work, or just work marginally, after investing a lot of time, money and resources into it. This happens in a lot of cases.

Business leaders have become frustrated at what is happening online, and now they are feeling more and more powerless as time rolls around. Despite taking that course on SEO, Facebook training and workshops, and learning how to run a group on Linkedin, they still cannot get any traction in what they are doing for their business. How does it all fit together? How do I increase my level of success online?

From the consumer perspective, and B2B, they simply do not care about individual businesses. It is the brutal reality, but it is the truth. "What's In It For Me", or, WIIFM, is the new buzzword that fundamentally affects businesses online. Your business is in essence, invisible to most, with people not really caring whether or not you actually exist.

"What's in it for me (WIIFM)? The new mantra for online."

These are some of the biggest problems that are occurring online that are negatively affecting how business is getting done.

It is not just about "building an engaging community", either, as most have come to realise. When businesses have a sizeable community, are they actually getting more sales? Are they getting more downloads of their app? Many new bookings yet?

How are you and your business actually "converting" your activities into revenue for your business?

What is the Return on Investment for your online business? If any one took an ROI measurement of the performance of a specific business, most would not have ever started down this path. Businesses have been deluded into thinking that they just need to "build it and customers will come". How is success measured? How will businesses know when they get there? Is there a scorecard that will help map things out?

The web is an influencer and decision tool; you need to actively be front and centre along the complete journey that your customer is taking. What you are doing in the beginning, ultimately will affect every single stage along the "buying" cycle - whether it is for an actual product that is sold, a download, an event, or whatever the type of business. Furthermore, the buying cycle or sales funnel really is not as linear as we were taught, or had hoped?

Any online business is no different in essence than their bricks and mortar counterpart. It is about building customer relationships, but also having an understanding of what works and what doesn't, and a framework to hold it all together.

> **"Do I really know what is happening online, to positively affect my business? Have I made an honest effort to look behind the facade of 'online.'"**

Let's be clear, this book is not just for the struggling or an emerging business online. It is for business leaders who want to stay relevant in the burgeoning online world. Many businesses may already have a Facebook page and an online website. This book is not to convince you to be online; you already know this quite intuitively. Businesses need to re-engage, as things just do not seem to be working as well as they should be. Right now, you may be feeling overwhelmed and under-utilised; but you want to build your online empire.

You may be starting to get your orientation in what needs to be done. You want some action to happen. You want things to grow. You want to get to that tipping point or create the momentum that will build a business breakthrough. You want to be the leading business that people will come to when they want to deal with someone. While this will certainly help in creating some realignment to your core business, it is also a reflection on what everyone needs to address in growing their business to the next level and building the business breakthrough that is out there.

If you are a seasoned online "pro", or part of the industry itself, and think you already "know all the answers", this book will help you further enhance and maximise what you are getting out of it, by building a new understanding and a new perspective to what you can do differently to squeeze that extra bit of value out of your business. Through years of online work, I have been able to identify some of the things that are inadvertently slowing businesses down, and more importantly, what entrepreneurs can do about it to get that extra value that is there. By reading and understanding the Framework, you will be able to gain additional traction, and move more your audience into your sales funnel for additional sales and business growth. This book will help you "tweak" things to becoming a fine running machine. It will show you what you need to continue to build your audience, as well as make you aware of critical aspects that you just may be missing.

Of course, many seasoned pros truly believe they know what you are doing. It is my belief that many businesses are part of this delusional mentality;

Do you have a sound and strong strategic digital business platform that will grow and sustain your business for the present and the future?

the perspective that feels that nothing is actually wrong, and that "I know everything". Some will choose not to read this book, as they will simply not be able to accept what is wrong with the current state of affairs. So, go ahead; put this book down now.

If you are a bricks and mortar business, and not online yet, or still waiting for the right time, this book will also help you get started. It will outline the delusions that are affecting existing online businesses, and the "groupthink" that is slowing others down. You will be able to take these lessons learned, apply the unique framework, and build a very strong foundation to grow your empire online.

This book is for the business leader and entrepreneur who is aware they need to get control of what is happening, and knows they are ready to make changes in what they do and how they get things done online. Regardless of who you are, or where your business is at, this book will cut through all the clutter, misguidance and misinformation that everyone has been subjected to in this ever growing online domain. It will simplify what is core to creating a strategy that combines all of the key, functional areas, and will deliver this in a unique 7 step framework that will actually allow you to get things done for your business. This as a working, functional book that will give entrepreneurs the hands on activities to actively engage in all of the critical online areas, it will help you find the focus that you need for your business to lead in its field.

This digital or online framework is called, "The Online Empire Project", and was designed from the ground up to address the common mistakes that are being made by most businesses online. It will detail the best way to create integration across all of the many areas of online business that exist. Everything that entrepreneurs need to know to build their business, has been condensed into a unique, 7 Frames process that will create the change that you are looking for, for your business. While the process created is meant to be somewhat linear and consecutive so that entrepreneurs can walk through each day, day by day, you are also able to jump into the framework at any time and at any stage, depending on the maturity of your business. That being said, completing each step or day in a consecutive fashion, allows you to truly build on the knowledge base that the previous day enabled.

A sound tool kit has been created to produce a strategy that defines who you are as the persona of your brand. All of the key components needed to make a difference, are then integrated to elevate your relevance online.

This book is not going to mire entrepreneurs through the infinite details of how to create the best Facebook post ever, or what to put in a video SEO box; it is about creating a relevant framework that allows you to move beyond the digital delusions that are affecting how you are running your business online. It is about learning what is right for your business. Facebook, like so many other social networks, is nothing but a tool that can be used.

At the end of the day, this is what all entrepreneurs are trying to achieve:

1. Reach the correct audience
2. Engage with relevant content
3. Motivate their audience to take a desired action
4. Spend efficiency
5. Deliver significant ROI

These are all tenets of a successful business, regardless of where it is located, what it does or how it is done. These are what are being forgotten in this "new" media maelstrom. This book will deliver this for those who have the courage to make the change that they know needs to happen, and the heart to understand that they will get the job done. There is no "half-way" with online businesses; you are either online or not. Stop being the "not". However, you do need to do more than just show up.

At this stage, you and your business are looking for key questions that need to be answered in all of your current online activities. These are illustrated by:

1. How do I overcome the clutter of online information, the social media hype, the overwhelming technologies, misguidance and misinformation online, to create business success by building an online empire so that it stands out from everyone else?

How do you define and measure success online?

2. How do I organise and leverage my business effectively online to connect with my audience, increase sales, get loyalty from customers, to get the business breakthrough I need and build my online empire?

3. As an entrepreneur, how do I find the right online business strategy to get my audience energised and engaged online, to help build my online empire and online business breakthrough?

The strategy in this book will help you solve these questions, for you and your business.

You will learn how to take your business from its current state, and create a dynamic breakthrough online, based on the unique and innovative framework presented. Through this process, you will cut through the glut of information that is out there and be able to focus on what is important for you to be successful online. The Online Empire Building Project Framework will walk you through each of the 7 core components that will distill everything that is fundamental to how you operate online. The easy to understand format and segregation of information will show you all the steps needed to re-engage your audience if you are already online, or develop a strong community foundation from the start, if you are just moving online. You will be able to align your strategy online with the essence of your business, creating the necessary congruency to build trust with your audience in the online world.

Throughout the chapters, there are specific objectives and tasks that need to be completed. These will allow you to further develop not just a conceptual answer from the text, but rather an actual working, functioning plan. At the conclusion of the book, you will then be able to assemble all of the necessary components into an over-riding plan. This will form your new and captivating strategy for your business. Additionally, the 7 Frames Online Empire Building Project Framework allows you to proceed, step by step, through each of the components that will then further develop a working plan that can actually be implemented.

By understanding the 7 Deadly Digital Delusions, and engaging in the Online Empire Building Project, you will create that connection that currently does not exist - not only with your business and your customer, but also with you and your business. You will create relevance with your audience that you did not have before. You and your business will resonate deeper, you will be able to attract and grow your audience versus simply interrupting them. Of course, from the business perspective, you will become much more effective and cost efficient online.

You won't be invisible any more.
This book is about what most businesses don't know, yet. This is what they need to know, now. If you could build a business that would truly engage and embrace your audience, would you do it?

This is not about convincing you that online is "good for you"; you already know that. This is about showing you how to get the job done, to your satisfaction, to make you the leader in your industry; plain and simple.

You are here, because you are not sure where to start, or what to do next. It is a symptom of fear sometimes. However, this strategy is going to lead you, so that YOU can do what you need to do, to get the breakthrough and success you need in your business.

A word to the wise - this will not be an easy thing that can just be picked up and completed, then left alone. Being online needs to be integrated into everything that you do, as part of your business. It does not matter what your business is about, you need to invest the time, money and resources to get the job done, and done properly. If you approach this development as just some "guidelines", and that you don't really need to do anything other than understand it, then this will not work for you, and you shouldn't be reading this. Again, put the book down and walk away. You will not be able to grow your business and build your online empire without the time-consuming, committed effort to get the job done properly, and become prolific. You just need to do it smarter than everyone else. Now is your chance!

Do you want to be the leader in your industry? Do you want to have a truly remarkable business? Do you want to stay relevant to your audience? Do you want to be visible? You need to rethink what is wrong with the industry as a whole; identify specifically what is incorrect and misguided, and make steps that put everything back into perspective, and more importantly, put you back in control, as opposed to being distracted by this tip and that network, etc.

This is what the Digital Delusion is about - not being afraid to identify what is wrong, and how to make it better; how to build a business breakthrough; how to build your own, online empire. This strategy will give you the tools that you need to get there.

So, let's get started.

"Adding sound to movies would be like putting lipstick on the Venus de Milo."

- Mary Pickford, silent movie star, 1925

The Beginnings

Being online is not just about having a business that stretches around the world, as this is not what every business leader wants; being online is also about building a strong business just around the corner from your customer. This is where we start.

What exactly is a delusion? A delusion is a false belief that persists despite it being at variance with the facts.

The Digital Delusion is about turning people's own misconceptions and misbeliefs, whether self-generated or industry-lead into discoveries of truth and certainty. It is about developing a strong sense of reality that works with online businesses.

The Digital Delusion is also defined by an overwhelming industry deception, equivocation, evasion, fallacies, and yes, even lies. These are generated from the industry itself, as well as the unscrupulous people that are in effect "pulling the wool over your eyes". It is prevalent everywhere. There is no escaping it, unless entrepreneurs are given the knowledge to be able to judge for themselves, and make their own decisions about what is best for their business.

Don't get me wrong, it's not all intentional either, but this is how the industry has evolved. These are the various behaviours that are exhibited practically everywhere.

The simple fact is, that most business leaders know that they can be successful; they just need the expertise and more importantly confidence to be able to build their online empire. There are no surprises here. Simply understand what you need to know, and how it will make a difference in your business. It's as simple as that; you are the expert. There are no secrets that need to be revealed, no special formula or secret recipe that will dictate your success online. This is all part of the digital delusion; you've been led to believe that this is a mysterious world, where only wizards, magicians, hypnotists, and illusionists know what they are doing. This strategy will give you all the tools you need to be able to build your business, to build your online empire.

It can be seen everywhere. The marketing towards this is all interruption, and in your face. "Want to be at the top of Google... then buy my 12 secrets"; "We'll give you 10,000 ways to get 10,000 fans... without breaking a sweat"; and my favourite "I just made $24,328 in my sleep last night". We have all seen these. We are all tired of these schemes. We all know they do not work, yet we still seem to cling to the belief that maybe, just maybe, "If I buy that one course to 'master my leads', then I will be set".

The reality is, this doesn't work. It's just too much to take in, adding to the clutter. Many believe they can't be successful or a leader online, that it takes eons of knowledge, and that perhaps it is even a bit magical in what it does. It is only mysterious because we have let ourselves believe that it is. It will only get worse if we let it. Only you can stop it: you as the entrepreneur, the business-leader that is ready to make the difference.

Everyone is tired of the deceptions. It's time to stop the suffering and do it on our own or move forward. It's time to get past the delusions to build your online empire.

What You Need to Actually Read This Book

No, this is not being sarcastic. This books is going to rely on several things:

1. Technology
2. Attitude
3. Implementation (Getting Sh*t Done)

We can direct you to what technology you need to embrace through this business transformation, your attitude cannot be adjusted. As we will state throughout the book, and as you are obviously starting to get the feel for, online work is difficult and time consuming, and resource intensive.

You need to be able to make the commitment up front that this is important for you and your business. It is important that your business becomes the best possible; we want you to be able to build your online business breakthrough.

We want you to build your online empire; and this is going to take some work and commitment on your part. You will need to dedicate time to completely read the book, engage in all of the activities, as well as interact and share online and offline.

The book and framework presented is fairly clear and straightforward; read it and understand that your business will not survive without you as the core, and will be enhanced by putting everything together for you.

Why are we telling you this? We want you to succeed. This framework has been developed as part of a solid business strategy that will make things happen for you and your business. You need to make things happen, and this strategy will help you do that.

You need to implement, to be proactive and productive or to get shit done, so to speak. No one is going to do it for you. Attitude is a choice, so change it and move forward; make things happen.

Connecting & Sharing With This Book

This book is not intended just for reading, it is a catalyst for action. It is about digital media, so readers absolutely need to embrace this. While the copy that you may be reading could in fact be a book printed on paper, we want to extend that into the digital world.

We want you to help us connect what you see and do with both versions of the book, in your own online community.

If you are reading the hard copy of this book, statistics show that more than likely you are within 50cm of your smart/mobile phone. It's probably sitting on the desk beside you, in your pocket, or on the armchair. So, take it out; you're going to be using it.

We're connecting this paper bound book into something that can be viewed online, something that you can interact with, and something that you can share and talk about. You will have the opportunity to "share" throughout the book - nominating the parts that you like and those that you might disagree with. You can connect wherever, and whenever you are.

Despite what format you are using, we want to create a book that allows that transition between the digital and "paper" media worlds. We want you to share and join our community, online. It's not perfect yet, but it will get there.

We will be using a variety of channels and technologies throughout the book. This will be a living and breathing example of working and collaborating between online and offline.

Of course the easiest one that you will see is simply the html links. These links will direct you to the page, or the specific resources that are referred to. You will also notice a variety of the QR Codes throughout the book. Scanning them will take you directly to the specific content that you are asked to refer to.

The digital experience will only be enhanced by using what is provided to you, in this flat, non-dimensional, book world. You will only be able to add that extra dimension by engaging the digital side of this book.

How To Get the Most from this book

If you want to get the most from this book, there are several things that you can do. Some sections can be read out of sequence. If you want to get right down to work, start with Chapter 7 where the details of the 7 Frames Online Empire Project is discussed. This is the new digital platform to get your business working online.

This book will take you on a new journey. It will tell your story from the beginning, and develop it into something contemporary and remarkable for your business. This is a joint venture that we will take, so that you can understand how everything fits together for you and your business.

Ready to implement? Ready to understand?

Here is how the book is broken down:

Chapters	What It's About	What You Can Do
Chapters 1, 2 & 3	Get you re-started	Gives a broad understanding of the actual thoughts behind the digital delusion
Chapter 4 & 5	The Main Foundation and Business Models	Understanding the main business model that will set up the necessary framework
Chapter 6	Setting up the framework	The key ingredients needed to establish the upcoming framework
Chapter 7 & Resources	Finishing touches	The various tools required for complete success; how to put an action plan together and "what to do next"

Terminology

There are some key words that will be used interchangeably throughout this book. Do you need to know them? Yes, but don't worry, there will not be a test on them at the end of this program. Consider the following perspectives:

1. Audience: The group of people that you are marketing to, that can potentially be your customer, or is already your customer. Some people may not necessarily be your target customer, but may still be

in your audience. Think of this scenario like a musical conductor - everyone listens, but not everyone will necessarily come for the same reasons.

2. Customer: People who are paying or paid for your products or services.

3. Digital Domain: No, this is not your website URL. This is everything that you and your business are about, online. It is your entire digital footprint. It is what connects everything to everyone; it is your "inter-tubes". Are you the master of your digital domain? Well you need to be.

4. Products: What you offer as a business. This also includes "services", such as consulting services, professional services etc. Why classify services as products? Primarily because creating a product from your services provides a much broader aspect of your offering, and allows you to increase your product offering substantially.

5. Visuals: The photographs and images that provide references to our visual worlds. Everything that is used, as "collateral" that is part of the overall visual message that we are delivering online.

6. Channel: A specific type of media, for example, television. Facebook, Google+, Twitter, etc. are all separate "channels". Your website is also considered a channel. It is important to understand that these channels can work together, but also how they need to create a "micro-habitat" on their own as well, as your audience may only be introduced to you through one specific channel at a time, until they get to know you further.

7. Keywords: All the words that are specifically related to your business and what you do online. Ideally, you should have a list of 6-10 "key" or significant words that are part of the over riding structure of how you explain to people what your business is about. Ensure you use these words regularly, in all of your content and descriptions, as it begins to build relevance to you and your website.

8. Digital Platform/Framework: The over-riding structure that encompasses all of your digital assets. It is everything you are a part of online, and that is part of your business. This is your strategy, content

and all the supporting activities that will be used to build your digital business. Creating your digital platform is the focus of this book.

9. Business Owners v. Business Leader v. Entrepreneur: A business owner works "in the business"; business leaders and entrepreneurs have made the transition to be able to work "on the business".

> "Have other definitions that are not always that clear? Please help me define others for you. Discuss them online"
> www.thedigitaldelusion.com/1

My Digital Journey So Far

Working in the online and e-commerce world for over 10 years, from the very early days of being online, has taught me a number of key principles and understandings. I have come through the entire evolution of online growth and change – from the original brochure websites to high level social media marketing campaigns and everything in between.

There have been many marketing campaigns and online strategies in which I can see what works. Not just what works, but what once worked and what doesn't work anymore. I have seen what's starting to work, and in the future what will work. I am so close to this online realm that I know all the history and also know what is coming up next.

I have worked with some massively big companies, like Samsung, Virgin Mobile, Toshiba, Skoda, Suzuki, Blackmores, and created one of the fastest growing online companies in Canada. All of this has helped me understand what we can deliver, but also the disconnect that exists online.

The problem with most businesses is that they get so caught up doing the day-to-day "things" to run their business, which they forget that they are in the most technologically, revolutionary times in history. They simply forget that most of the tools online are in fact designed to help businesses get the word out and spread their marketing information directly to the market place – their audience. You have probably heard it before, but most business owners are working "in" the business; whereas the transformation to a business leader or entrepreneur, means that you work "on" your business.

More importantly, the biggest problem is that many entrepreneurs are not quite sure what they don't know, and what they need to be doing, so they simply ignore it. This turns into a huge problem for businesses.

I find it so frustrating to see businesses flounder today, as they miss tremendous opportunities in front of them. They could be doing so much more.

It's been said that there are hundreds of email marketers, Internet marketers, online gurus, SEO wizards, and all that sort of stuff, and that it's simply not worth paying any attention to them. It's true that in every industry there is good and bad. The underlying truth is that we are going through a massive transformation, and some people will benefit and some will not. There are good people who will help you benefit and there are those who won't.

The real reason behind this book and everything else I do, is that I have a passion for the Internet, the marketing, and the strategies that make it all work, and of course, entrepreneurship and what you can do with it. Think Digital innovation and entrepreneurship. With my background, I could have taken my passion and channeled it into absolutely any field and any industry that I enjoyed and loved. However, when I really analysed and realised what this transforming technology was moving ahead to do, I understood that small businesses were the hottest place where this was going to happen. This is "the" place for an incredible opportunity, and the ground zero for the biggest impact for all things entrepreneurial.

I wanted to be right there, to see and watch people's faces light up when they "get it", when they realise that it now changes their life and their business. When they see that "ah-ha" moment that makes revolutionary changes for them, then things start to fall in place, and they then understand how this will change their lives, and the lives of those around them.

What is digital innovation and entrepreneurship? How important are they on your day to day business?

The mission for me is not about the software, not about the social media, or the techno-babble of it all; it's about seeing people reach that moment when they realise how everything comes together. I believe that this stuff has the capabilities to free up people's time. If we all have more time, we can all be more successful, and then we can really start tackling the bigger problems that need attention.

Doyle Buehler

I want to educate people on what is going on in the online world. This book is designed to do just that - give you and your business an extra hand for you to "get it"; for you to truly put everything in place with what your original dream was all about.

I am known for making complex online digital systems easy to use and simple to understand; systems that are suitable for small businesses. From interacting with this strategy, people are left feeling like they are a true online empire builder.

The development of this overall strategy and the 7 digital delusions was multifold. For awhile, when someone would ask for help or assistance in search engine optimisation, paid search advertising, social media, website development, or whatever it was that they needed, they would always seem to have their blinkers on for how everything actually fit together and how all aspects linked and worked together. Many questions were raised, and nothing was connected. But to everyone, it seemed as though that was ok, that it didn't really matter.

The delusions continued. The industry was far too segregated at this stage. Entrepreneurs are not naive. They know there is always a better way. This book will help point all entrepreneurs in the right direction, in a direction that has the capability to move their business forward, dramatically, to become the leader in their industry.

There are a lot of books on the shelves of thousands of bookstores, and millions of book owners. There is no shortage of books about online business, SEO this, Social Media that... ecommerce here, adwords there. "Dummies" everywhere it seems. The most significant thing that really came to mind that was missing from all of these books, was organisation and order. Too many books are all over the place, with little focus on the core problem. The core issue was always diluted with technologies and babble – not the foundation of what is needed to actually build a strong business. Others continue to perpetuate the delusion with information that is irrelevant, out of context, and has no simple framework to keep all the different pieces fitting together. I almost always felt more confused after reading these sorts of books. There is obviously a need for these different

12   THE DIGITAL DELUSION

levels of books, as they do help – there just wasn't anything that actually tied this all together. All of this is about to change right now with this book. The delusions are definitely real - but you can overcome them to become the leader in your industry.

I want to help you build that strategic alignment and online integration as well, so you and your business can reach spectacular growth. This is why I created the Online Empire Project, and communicating it through the story of The Digital Delusion. Once you have implemented and mastered this process, you will be able to do what you love - grow and dominate with your business.

Enjoy discovering your digital delusions and revealing your new reality. Your new empire.

Doyle Buehler

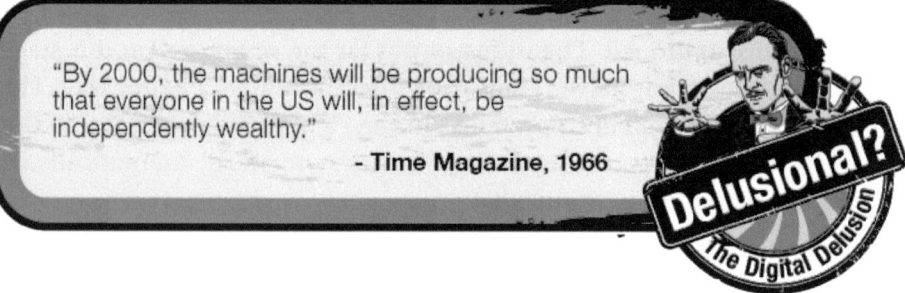

Discover some additional insights and what you can learn about your digital business. Scan QR Code or Link here: www.thedigitaldelusion.com/1

"By 2005 or so, it will become clear that the internet's impact on the economy has been no greater than the fax machine's."

- Paul Krugman, Economist, 1998

State of the Affairs

You have all heard it before:

> "Business online is moving at a frightening pace. What you learned yesterday no longer applies today. What you will learn tomorrow, will not apply the following day. You really don't stand much of a chance to be able to actually build and grow a business online. You might as well give up now, as you are not going to get anywhere, nor make any money".

It's really no different than the late night infomercials, hocking the latest extraordinary knife set, or "1-second ab-buster revolution". This is the obvious level of "crap" that is constantly inundating everyone and every business online. You simply can't escape it, until now. Nothing really gets results from misinformation and misguidance. Do you really know what the html <alt> tag is for, or more importantly, why you should actually care? We are awash in the guru-speak and buzz word death that leaves nothing tangible to actually work with.

So, why then would you actually pick up a book and start to read, when it professes some "solution" that you have not heard of, nor seen before? Are you in fact delusional, like the title implies? You are curious; curious in the fact that something that seems so hard from the outset, can actually be quite easy - but only when it is shown in a step by step manner does it actually start to make sense. We've made it easy to connect the dots to the pieces that are important to your business.

Is there a safe haven? The first stage to recovery is recognition, as they say. Think of this as giving you the ability to recognise the self-perpetuating fraud of the entire online industry. This is about recognising everything that is preventing you from really making the progress that you should and need to be making. You are, in essence, being deluded into thinking that if you build your business, "they" will come. It is possibly that "they" in this context is in fact the bills and costs that must be endured without really seeing any return on your investment.

Yes, your ad agency will tell you everything you want to hear. The online world is a wonderful place. "We just want you to increase your spend by

15%, or maybe another $50,000 so that we can really, really get you the results that you need". The results never come. Yes, you get more traffic perhaps, but typically it is proportionally less than the 15% that you just invested. Your consultant will tell you that you now need to spend $5000 per month so that they can "really" optimise your SEO. Optimise? More like lobotimise, taking your brain and your wallet.

There is no accountability online. No responsibility. No leadership. It's a big free-for-all, however, people and businesses are losing money. It's not a gold rush, despite what you have been told, this is a delusion.

It's not all rose gardens out there, with bright-shiny yachts, where everyone is becoming the next Richard Branson, or worse, the next Mark Zukerberg. There's lots of money to be made, but it's currently being made by your agency, your consultants, your so-called "experts", your "gurus".

Many have been "hypnotised" and "lobotomised" into believing certain things about online and how it works; we have been deluded into thinking that the online world and the Internet is the next gold rush. Many of the "technologies" you need have been hidden, only to be revealed by the so called experts and gurus, who will tell you - but only if you are worthy, and if you can pay the price. It seems people will pay, as money is spent in this space like no other. The reality is that not everyone will know these "secrets" either. They can though, they can build their online empire if they are willing to recognise how they are being deluded, and what exactly they can do about this situation. The digital delusions are the perceived realities of the online business world; the strategy that you are about to embark upon is the map that will make the difference in your business world, wherever or whatever that may be.

Of the billions of dollars that are spent online, what does this actually equate to in real value? Where does this extra value go, or come from? Yes, unfortunately it comes from you and your business by simply overspending and not thinking twice, or by not demanding of the industry that you get a ROI that actually works with you and your business.

You need to ask yourself: How much money is my company spending on marketing and on online "work"? How much am I wasting? Or, how can I spend my marketing dollars so as to waste as little as possible. How can I best spend my digital marketing dollars for the greatest possible impact?

Like most business-leaders, you have more than likely taken your fair share of courses, workshops, seminars, etc. While you usually pick up a few tips here and there, again and again, you come back to square one in terms of how to fit it all together to actually make it work. Businesses spend thousands of dollars annually on training that really does not provide that intrinsic value, that complete ROI. Why is this? The complete picture, and step-by-step activities are never presented in a manner that makes sense and integrates everything that you need to know. You need to know everything; but you need to know it in a manner that actually works for you and your business.

Beyond the hemorrhaging of money onto the industry, the next brutal reality is that the online industry is more work than you can imagine. It is more time-consuming and resource dependent than you actually think it is. And, it is certainly not "easy". It has cost you, and fortunately, your competitors, an unimaginable amount of funding, with very little to show for. We can see the advertisements now... "I spent $12,498 and made $328 thanks to my [insert SEO, Social Media] expert". ROI? What's that? "We don't need a ROI as the industry is still in its infancy". This is something you have no doubt heard and have certainly come to believe. That in fact is the story behind the story - everything that you know about online business is, unfortunately, wrong.

> "What do you think of when you hear the term 'guru'? Are you studying yoga or digital marketing?"

Despite the digital doom and gloom delusions, there are some companies that are doing things right. There are some companies that are putting things together that work quite well for them and their business. What is the difference, then? Who is succeeding and who is failing? The ones who are succeeding have taken the time up front to understand what they need to accomplish, and have built an integrated strategy that approaches all of the elements, simultaneously. They understand that there is a bigger picture that they need to be aware of, and utilise. This is the "big picture" that the strategy in this book is going to give you.

Why is this any different then? The difference is that we understand that YOU are the expert in your business; what we will do is help you identify the problem areas that are causing you, your business and your audience significant pain. We are providing you with a framework to be able to effectively build what you need. As a business leader, you already know what your business is about; we simply extract this and place it into a format that allows you to leverage the information in the online environment; we take what you know, and put it into play in a format that makes sense. Anyone can do this.

You can buy a book trying to solve all of your problems online, but these always seem to leave out that connectedness that is so important. Deep down, you know it is important for your business, and you don't have to have an MBA to know this either. Many of these publications have forgotten to include the ability to build congruency and clarity between you, your brand and your content. They have forgotten that you need to create integration amongst all of the different silos that exist in everyone's online environment. They have forgotten that you need to define the essence of your brand in order to build the essence of your audience and community. They have forgotten about, you.

Empire Builders

Online empire building is not some term fabricated to make this whole book and process sound more important than it actually is. This term has been used throughout the book, and you are probably wondering what exactly does it mean? Now that you have a background about some of the basic processes, we will now be able to expand upon this, not as some meaningless term, but rather as an entrepreneurial philosophy, and how we actually function, and can leverage this concept.

Daniel Priestly, Best-Selling Author of Become a Key Person of Influence (2010), has developed a model that attempts to illustrate the various stages that all entrepreneurs go through. There is a mental "battle" to get to the level of success that we deem and "feel" is appropriate. We naturally tend to fall back into the patterns or chaos when we are not focused. This is the battle between our Reptile Brain, our Monkey Brain, and our Empire Building Brain.

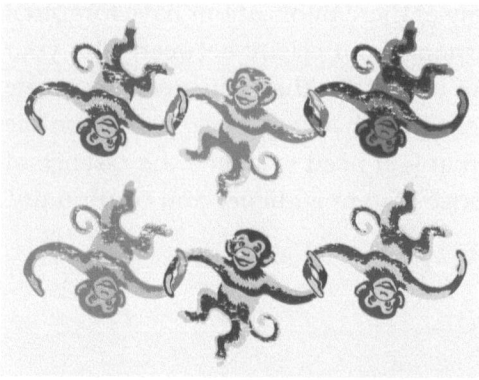

We all have a good reason to use our reptile and monkey brains. The questions is, can you use your empire building brain?
Which Brain Are You Using? Are You Feeding Your Monkey or Reptile Brain?

We can lose our focus when we feel desperate, out of control, and when we do not have a proper plan with our business. Where do we start? We start with something that has been with us for millions of years of human evolution, back to the days of lizards and other reptilian beasts. Even to this day, we can quickly revert back to the reptilian instinct. The reptilian behaviour is our fear of survival; the fear that what is available in terms of resources, will be depleted, and depleted quickly. We believe that everyone is there to steal our food, our lunch, and yes, even our business. We are quick to respond foolishly, and fear that we are constantly and consistently "losing out". We focus on picturing our severely limiting resources that everyone is seemingly after. We begin to horde, and do not reflect on the bigger picture. It is a basic survival mechanism, and it is there for a reason - to help us survive. As an entrepreneur, you need to do more than just survive.

This reptilian response is not part of our truly intellectual brain. It is our fight or flight response; one that may get the short-term goals, but consistently jeopardises long-term futures. It is the "get rich quick", or even better, "make money while you sleep", of the online domain. It is the immediate response to most things; we are prone to make bad decisions, for the most part of it. You are able to overcome this if you can focus on the bigger picture; your overall strategy. This is where thought processes need to be re-wired towards an ultimate goal, the ultimate focus of empire building. Understanding it, and acknowledging it for what it is, will be the only mechanism that enables you to overcome this impulsive behaviour.

Picking out these behaviours, as well as the people that are exhibiting them is quite easy. What does this look like? It can be seen in simple concepts that are displayed, like affiliate marketing through multiple streams of income, the one-big-win scenario, "make money online", the concept of "passive income", "getting huge traffic to your site", ad nauseum. The online world is full of these, and like many, have all fallen to it's charm of getting rich, creating immense traffic online, or having an immense email list where everyone supposedly responds quickly to...."And, all in 2 easy payments of $47! But wait, there is more...".

Affiliate marketing, and "internet marketing" are also misnomers, and need to be clarified. An affiliate program, when it is to sell and market a tangible product, such as your own goods and services, can be quite effective, and is a recommended feature of the Online Empire Project. Affiliate programs however, at least the legitimate ones, have gotten a bad wrap, because of unscrupulous marketers preying on the reptile brain of clients. The affiliate marketing, that promised the get rich quick, or any of the other crap that is sold online, needs to be avoided. There is no tangible product or service - just an idea that creates an immediate response. Think late night television info-mercials. As part of your online empire project, we will outline exactly how you can make affiliate marketing work for your business.

Internet marketing is also one of those words that means different things to those both inside and outside the industry. Marketing is everywhere, however, the type of marketing that is evolving online, verges on being illegitimate and is often designed to trigger a reptilian response. This type of marketing targets the lower end of the human response; it is geared towards that trigger that most respond to; of riches, saving time, money, traffic, etc. You can quickly identify these because this is all that they talk about; it is their sole content. It is no different than days of old with the unscrupulous salesmen hawking medicine oil. "Real" marketing online is being segregated into the legitimate side, "Online Marketing", and "Internet Marketing", implying the sales of goods and services designed for quick trigger responses.

Are you doing "real" internet marketing, or are you part of the problem? **How's That Internet Marketing Going For you? Is Your Paypal Account Full Yet?**

Internet marketing is very effective, as it immediately creates a response; you more than likely have responded to these types of offers as well, and may have a leaner bank account because of it. I know that I have fallen prey to this illusion. It is extremely frustrating when you constantly pour money into it for this program, ebook and that software, but it never produces concrete results. There are a lot of advertisements, both for online services and of course regular consumer products that all use this method. Why? It is known to work, and is a core human motivator; it "connects" with our reptilian "autoresponder". Many have made many so-called internet marketers rich.

The problem is that type of marketing is always short-lived, if it actually does work. It is never a long-term strategy, as it is used for that instantaneous response that triggers a certain need; that demonstration that everything is limited, and that we will miss out. While it can be effective at times (and, mostly for the one who is selling to you), it leaves most customers feeling emptied and somewhat cheapened by the experience. And no, no analogy required here, either.

Where does the brain head next, once we have overcome this reptilian response, with limited resource thinking, and the belief that we don't know where our next lunch is coming from? Well, if you are an evolutionist, you will know that our next closest evolutionary cousin is of course the monkey.

Our monkey brain is, in essence, the focus of the bright and shiny objects all around us. It is about our familiarity with things, our own comfort zone. It is about chasing our tails as we look for the next thing that will bring our success, the next thing that will help build our business. It is our compelling will to "act". If we just keep "doing things", we will get things done. It's about thinking that "busy" is something good and that everyone should just be "busy", as that way, something will get done. We really need to stop the glorification of "busy"; the actions are typically futile, as they have no real connection to where businesses truly want to go and how they are going to get there. We have all heard of the expression about a room full of monkeys with typewriters will (eventually) be able to type a novel. They weren't kidding when they said this, as you can quickly identify this behaviour in your business.

This is so-called viral marketing at it's finest. Think of the momentous "memes" that forever recirculate on the internet – bacon, babes and cats.

Is there such a thing as viral marketing? Are you able to recreate it? **Look, it's the Viral Marketing Button - Push Button Now For Instant Success! Trust me now!**

www.TheDigitalDelusion.com

They are "bright and shiny", they are a distraction, and yes, they are hardly ever repeatable. They are brief in experience, and they are part of the 7 Deadly Digital Delusions. This is why they work so well, and why they get carried around the world within hours. We all like shiny things; amazingly, so do monkeys.

Overcoming these various stages of your thinking are extremely instrumental in the success of your business. How do you overcome them, and get to the Empire Builder, as part of your personality and better yet, behaviours? You need to readjust how you think and how you problem solve. You need to build a strong strategy for your business, you need to remove the self-perpetuating distractions, you need to work on your business, not in your business. This is how you change things.

You may think that you are "above all this", but sadly most are not. One of the key identifiers is quite simple - do you have a business strategy? Do you actually know what the "essence" of your business is? Do you find yourself putting out fires? Do you feel overwhelmed by the information that is out there, and what you should do, could do, maybe need to do? When someone asks "how are you doing?" is your typical response "busy"? Most Business Leaders all do this. The powerful thing is that you can overcome this; you can focus on what is more important to your and your business.

So how do we get past the reptile response and the monkey brain? What is next? This is the domain where real business leaders lie. This is where the real changes take place. This is where the real entrepreneurs and the real leaders come forth. This is not just a place, but rather it is a way of thinking. Consider it the true meaning of entrepreneurship, as how we actually think about things is as important as how we do things.

It's not a magical, mysterious place inhabited by wizards and magicians or even illusionists. It's a place where we can unleash our true intuition, where we can trust, honour and respect everyone both in our circles, and outside. It is where we can actually create the influence that really matters.

This is the empire builder part of your brain. The part that embraces change, the part that actually relays it in a concept that is always constructive and always available. It is a state of mind, where all resources are there for you to take maximum advantage of. Not in the negative sense of pillaging and destruction, but rather that everything and anything is possible.

It is the way of thinking that your resources are available somewhere and somehow - you just need to actually find them, engage them and enable them. In this empire building mindset, you are able to leave behind the monkey and reptile brains and focus on the key tasks at hand.

Are you building your EMPIRE, or just watching other entrepreneurs build theirs? **Are Your Ready To Be an Empire Builder?**

Empire building online is no different. There are a myriad of problems, technical details and knowledge that can be quite detrimental to your own existence. You need to think like an empire builder online. This is where your success will come from.

How do you actually embrace this so-called 'Empire Builder'? You have to change your thinking, and avoid those choices that create an immediate response. You need to focus on the bigger picture, the one that says that you know there is bounty in your industry; and decide that your job is to extract this value. Imagine if you had unlimited resources, unlimited money, unlimited partners to help you. This is how you get started in empire building. If the way that you think is bountiful, you will attract high performing people, and you will be able to get the job done.

The Online Empire Project is what has been created in order to allow you to focus on what is important, and get rid of everything that is not. It allows you to build a sound strategy, and create an activity plan that keeps you on task. The strategic architecture that you will create as part of this framework, helps keep your business from wandering from project to project, and from

www.TheDigitalDelusion.com

social channel to social channel. It helps you define the purpose of you and your business in an easy to understand format. It basically kicks you in the ass! It tells you that you can shut down that reptilian response and the monkey moments, and gets you to lay a proper, key framework for your online empire, like a true entrepreneur.

You can of course build a business based on the reptile brain and the monkey brain. Think of, as mentioned, affiliate marketing, but also passive income based businesses, multiple streams of income, "retirement" based type businesses. These work; the problem is that they are only attracting those buyers and consumers who believe in the same thought patterns, the same behaviours that typically just keep them there. The good news is that there are businesses that occupy these domains, and they now don't need to be yours.

This is not a book about entrepreneurship; this is just a starting point for new ideas that will allow you to continue to develop your empire building Brain.

The Online Empire Project is a methodology or framework that allows you to build a strong strategy, create a strong plan and activities, and allows you to work on your business with higher ideals and solutions. It is built upon the over riding idea that in order to build an empire, you need to think like you will.

The Online Empire Project helps you get rid of distractions, and keeps the overwhelming feelings from overtaking you and what you do. You can use this project to jump-start your business, as well as keep you on course. It all starts with a strategy that works for you in the online world. This is Empire Building.

What kind of brain do you use?

How to discover if you have a reptilian brain or a monkey brain? Ask yourself some simple questions:

1. Have you ever bought an online "tool", ebook, software, or program to help you build traffic?

2. Have you ever "dabbled" in money-making affiliate marketing?
3. Have you ever "perked up" when you encounter a supposedly "newer" opportunity?
4. How many "big ideas" do you have going on at any moment?
5. How many times have you clicked on that "make money from home" ad?
6. How many ab-blasters, slap-chops and useless kitchen utensils do you own?

Are You The Master of Your Digital Domain?

Online business is not just about simple things like web design or making a website; it goes far beyond this. Most businesses that are already online have also realised this. You've added Facebook, you have a Twitter account, maybe even a Linkedin account. You've been to that SEO session and you have learned that you've got so much more to learn and do, that eventually you just stop doing it. You've stopped tweeting, you've stopped posting on Facebook, and you ignore all of those Linkedin requests. Why? You are overwhelmed by the rules, the technology, the theories, the guru-babble. "Do this, don't do that". How can you actually function?

You stop out of FEAR - fear of making a mistake, fear of doing something wrong. Fear of incorrectly connecting things that might actually bring down the entire Internet, immediately after which you will hear a knock on the door...

If someone clicks online, does anyone hear it?
Online, No One Can Hear You Scream.

A "typical" agency can come to be known about simply throwing money at the problem to see if a solution comes out of it. Whether it is an ad agency, SEO agency, web agency, social media agency, they do not know your business as well as you, and they are not motivated in the correct alignment to what is important to you and your business. Something not working? Need more "likes", more "traffic"? Well, just spend more money on it. While this is great for businesses with unlimited budgets, it doesn't work for the rest of the business world. You need to be smarter.

Despite spending money, most agencies still don't have an effective strategy to integrate a full and proper solution to the digital dilemma. They do advertising, SEO, social media; not strategy. They really don't understand what it means to actually build a business across the entire spectrum of needs to build a proper comprehensive digital platform, your "digital domain". They don't know how to create and build an architecture for your business; one that actually builds and grows organically; one that includes relevance and meaning. They are simply in it for the profit or money.

In reality, no one is listening to you online. Not even your supporting agencies. No one actually cares that you are online.

The Top 7 Mistakes Most Entrepreneurs And Businesses Make Online

Here's why businesses are not the master of their digital domains:

1. Not knowing what social channels to use and when. Not understanding how to use social media and the online market space.
2. Forgetting to follow a specific process for moving online, or developing an online presence and influence.
3. Thinking that your audience online actually cares about who you are or what you do, and will quickly engage and respond to what you have to say.
4. Not having a proper step-by-step plan telling people about themselves and their company online.

5. Not knowing what tools are easily available to make the process substantially easier.

6. Thinking that everyone already knows about your company and that your information is relevant.

7. Being reactive and unable to provide a clear focus, strategy and direction to building your online influence.

The Top 7 Problems That Most Entrepreneurs and Businesses Face Online

This comes from a misunderstanding of the problems that businesses encounter online. There is no easy solution; first you need to discover what it is that is going wrong. The online world is really quite ugly and unforgiving. Where do things start to go "wrong"? Do these sound familiar?:

1. Too much online apathy with customers. Customers are spending more time, money and resources with your competitors.

2. You have little to no influence online. People are simply not listening or seeing how great and remarkable you actually are.

3. There are never enough leads and committed people. You are unable to develop enough business and contacts to build or sustain your business.

4. No defined or clear strategy for working online exists. Bouncing around from idea to idea happens regularly. Putting out fires is your marketing plan. There is uncertainty of what exactly to do next.

5. Too much "noise" and clutter online. Too many distractions for your ideal customer to find you and engage with you.

6. Difficulty in finding the "right" customer for your market; the customer who is truly intrigued by what you offer.

7. Confusion with all of the different tools, activities, and types of social media channels. Too many things to consider making any one thing work well. Falling behind in what tools are available for marketing.

How do you master your digital domain? You first learn how to understand the problems that are encountered online, and then you need to create a proper framework for your business.

The Digital Delusion Manifesto

I believe that the time for building and establishing your online strengths now are critical for the overall success of your business for years to come. If you do not move online properly and with a clear plan, your business will fail and die. Imagine being the leader online with your business, and having a clear framework to work with. Having a clear strategy and proper implementation will allow you to stay years ahead of your competition, and strengthen and grow your customer base. The businesses that get this right now will be able to reap the benefits and successes and continue to build their business from strength to strength. Everyone has the power and fortitude to be successful with their business online - they just need to be able to see the forest through the trees; they need to be able to create the passion online.

Online business is not easy, and it is going to take a lot of work. It is a very competitive industry, there is so much clutter, and you need to be prepared to fully commit to the game. It's do or die. You can become the successful business entrepreneur that makes a difference online; the entrepreneur who has customers around the world and is a genuine success and dynamic leader in your industry. Now you can make your goals happen, you can make a difference with your business, you can live the life that you want and are working towards. I believe that you can fully reach your goals. What do you believe? What do you want to be known for?

The Digital Delusion Manifesto

Isn't it amazing that you can literally be in touch with thousands and thousands of customers, from around the world, 24 hours a day? You can access these customers wherever and whenever you are working, or not working for that matter.

It is time to understand what the industry is, and how it has evolved. Do you want to continue down the path where you don't actually know where you are going or what it is all for? How will you get to where you want to go? How will you measure success?

Don't you want to have a business that works through the problems, step by step, in a logical and methodical manner?

Do you want to actually feel that you are working with the system or against it? This is what the digital delusion is about - overcoming what we fear the most, and that which in the way it is presented to us. The online industry is very young, and it is developing in the direction that is not conducive to business. It is not conducive to being smart, it is not conducive to being an entrepreneur.

It is being built like so many systems and methodologies of the past, in our very tall silos, our tall individual towers, with little regard of the interdependencies of all aspects. These systems have failed in the past, and they will fail now. The industry is starting to see the cracks - the delusions that we all need to overcome. We need to break them down so that we can build our empire to get back to what we love - our business, and our lifestyles.

Now is your time to discover what you really need. We have taken everything that is right and everything that is wrong, and made it into something that you can do! This needs to be done or we will be no further ahead in five years time. We need to re-create an industry that is based upon relevance and integration. This will move you forward.

www.TheDigitalDelusion.com

You can tear down the industry in the way that it currently exists. You can then take advantage of it by refocusing and making it work for you. Understand the delusions and you will be able to reshape the industry in the way that it actually works for you, not against you.

We don't need the silos of SEO, SMM, PPC, and everything else out there. We don't need agencies to tell us what to do to spend our money and to leave us with few, if any, results. We don't need someone else to run our business.

Now is the time to become accountable for your own business, online.

Now is the time to get involved. To work it. To understand it. And, to get the job done. The tools to make it happen, and to get the job done are available. This is where it starts.

Stop taking everything for granted; pull your head out of the sand, and own your industry online. Understand the process behind it all, and commit to the results, commit to a clear understanding, commit to getting the job done, commit to getting involved. Question those who think they know, those who you are paying to know, and those who think they know. Question everything, now.

This is your business, and only you know it. This is where you have an advantage over every other business out there, and every other business that is trying to get in front of you. This is your business. Not theirs.

Online is changing, and you can be at the front of this change. Right now, you are standing where the world will start to pivot, online. You will be at the front of the pivot, only because you have recognised that there is a clear solution, that there is a new process that will actually work for you, not against you or your business.

Now is the time to make a difference, now is the time to take your business to the next level. Now is the time where you can become the leader and everything will follow after you.

The businesses that continue to focus on one aspect only online, will be the businesses that continue to fail.

You have the opportunity to truly make a difference with your business; to make your business work the way that you know it should be working.

Find the tools that work, and the underlying strategy that will make a difference in your business.

There has never been a better time to make a difference online.

You are ready to make the change. You are ready to change the industry. You are ready to change the way that you do business online.

We have to be smarter online, not just spending more and more money. We're tired of throwing our profits away.

We are motivated to discuss the problems of the online world, the digital delusions, and to put something together that works. We are about being the pioneers of building the congruency needed to be industry leaders. We are about implementing a solid strategy for all businesses that want great success.

The Digital Delusion is an "anti" agency. It is a way of doing business. It is a new way of thinking and implementing for businesses wanting to become leaders in their industry.

We are creating a new awareness and understanding of what is needed to succeed online. It is about mastering the digital domain and creating clarity and confidence online, for your business.

It is about helping entrepreneurs and business leaders cut through the clutter and confusion of being online, to become remarkable.

It is about time.

There has never been a better time to build my online empire.

"Remote shopping, while entirely feasible, will flop because women like to get out of the house, like to handle merchandise, like to be able to change their minds."
— Time Magazine, 1966

Download the Manifesto as a poster to hang in your office.
Scan QR Code or Link here: www.thedigitaldelusion.com/1

> "New Coke [will be] the most significant soft drink development in the company's history... the surest move ever made."
>
> — Roberto Goizueta, Coca-Cola Company chairman on their beverage flop, 1985

What You Need To Know

This chapter defines the Digital Delusions, and helps you understand what they actually are and how they are affecting you and your business.

You will learn:

1. The specific behaviours and beliefs of the online industry that are affecting your business.

2. How to identify other industry delusions that are affecting you and your business.

3. How to leverage what you are doing.

4. How you and your business currently fit into a "delusion".

The Digital Delusions

What are the digital delusions, what do they mean, and how do they affect you and your business? The 7 Deadly Digital Delusions are categorised by specifically identifying each one, followed by ways to "defeat them". You will be provided with a means to simply identify these delusions and create a way to confront them head on so that you can overcome them. There is nothing complicated about it, you will just recognise exactly what is holding you back from doing things the way you need to get them done.

The delusions are easily overcome by putting you in charge of everything, and becoming accountable. In the Online Empire Building Project in Chapter 7, we further reinforce what you and your business need to accomplish to actually fully overcome the delusions.

Each and every business might interpret these "delusions" differently. We would love to hear what you have found to be the "delusional" that is being experienced by your business. Join the discussion on the delusions that you know exist.

Jot down your thoughts and ideas; the ones you think are important to stop the misinformation and misguidance.

My Digital Delusions

_____

_____

_____

_____

_____

_____

_____

Are You Delusional? The Mini-Audit

The mini-audit was designed to be a quick indicator as to where you and your business currently stand in the online environment. While some questions are quite subjective, it is meant to give you an idea of where things are at with you and your business.

This doesn't mean that you are delusional or not - it is really just a quick indicator of where you think things are at. There is no right or wrong answer, to say the least. It will help you gauge where you are at, so that you can build your own individual, unique plan for your business, using our 7 Frames Online Empire Framework.

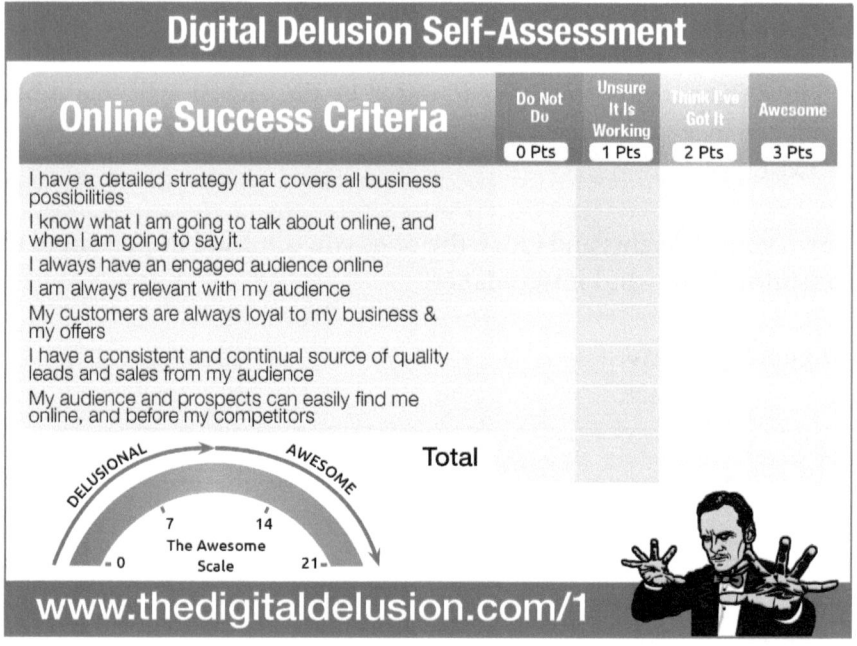

Take the Digital Delusion Self-Assessment to Discover What You May Need To Improve

Regardless of whether you are completely, and amazingly 'awesome', you still can learn an awful lot from this book to propel your business forward, online. This strategy will help you master your digital domain.

What Defines a Delusion?

You can let out a sigh of relief now, even though we are just getting started. The good thing is that we are not necessarily talking about the psychiatric definition of delusional, in terms of madness. We all know that every one, is quite sane, and completely functional mentally.

We have all heard the expression, "delusions of grandeur". Delusions are difficult to diagnose.

What starts out as a seemingly rational belief, is further perpetuated into irrational thought. Not from our selves but more from the onslaught of the inundation of information; it is difficult to actually discern what is right and what is wrong; what is relevant and what is not.

Online has really moved from the rational to the irrational, based on misconceptions and mis-guidance. The problem has self-perpetuated, due to a lot of common, shared beliefs by entrepreneurs and others wanting to leverage online.

de·lu·sion (dĭ-lōō'zhən)
n.
1.
    a. The act or process of deluding.
    b. The state of being deluded.
2. A false belief or opinion: *labored under the delusion that success was at hand.*
3. *Psychiatry* A false belief strongly held in spite of invalidating evidence, especially as a symptom of mental illness: *delusions of persecution.*

[Middle English *delusioun*, from Latin *dēlūsiō, dēlūsiōn-*, from *dēlūsus*, past participle of *dēlūdere*, to delude; see **delude**.]

de·lu'sion·al *adj.*

The American Heritage® Dictionary of the English Language, Fourth Edition copyright ©2000 by Houghton Mifflin Company. Updated in 2009. Published by Houghton Mifflin Company. All rights reserved.

The words, "The Digital Delusions" were coined because we really wanted to get to the bottom of how behaviours and beliefs can actually be changed, so that entrepreneurs can escape the reptilian response and the monkey moments, and focus on their online empire.

What are the 7 Deadly Digital Delusions?

A lot of time has been spent looking at what is currently happening in the online industry. Not just considering aspects as an outsider, but also as an insider; an insider into online business, as well as media agencies, consulting and the mind of the entrepreneur.

Being scared of being online, or at least admitting being scared, is the premise of this entire concept of the "Deadly Digital Delusions". In conversation after conversation with many entrepreneurs, it was becoming clear that there simply were a lot of things that people believed that simply were not true. Like most things, there really were some massive levels of generalisation that seemed to capture most of the people in it's wake. Things like, "I only need to be online and I will be successful", or "my site will make money once it is up". These are huge generalisations that in the end were causing significant grief for business owners and consumers alike.

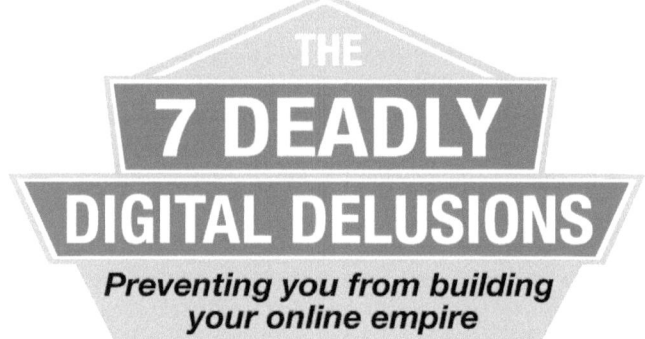

What factors are affecting the success of your business? How are you defining them, so that you can actually do something about them?

Yes, delusional is what we are talking about here. This is the unending belief that something is true, despite the inordinate amount of "real" information ascertaining the actual facts. We can all be deluded at times.

Many business-leaders were simply accepting the "good word" from the so-called experts, gurus, media, success stories, etc. but had left the "relevant" thinking at home. They were not prepared to actually discover what was meant by all the online stuff, and just accepted it as it was, without questioning it. This is where the difficulties lie - deciding that you can't possibly know enough to be able to create your own knowledge base, or that it is "too hard for me to understand, therefore I will leave it in the hands of the more trust worthy people". This just doesn't work. This is your business.

The biggest problem is the misinformation and misguidance that almost self-perpetuates, and more so, is perpetuated by those "experts" with more mis-information; it is really a vicious spiral. Yes, a lot of misguidance comes from self-professed "gurus" and the like, who want to impress with what they know, but a lot also comes from ourselves, too. Ourselves in the sense of our own limiting beliefs, but also from the "mob" that we call social media. Facebook, for example, is almost always awash with self-generated privacy statements, copyright notices and the like. As true entrepreneurs, you must become more accountable for your own digital platform.

Online business development is hard. It is however, no harder than building a strong business elsewhere. It just takes some key understandings and a fair amount of work to make it happen. If you have the proper understanding, a good foundation and framework, then it will become easier to accomplish and navigate. We all know this, but most of the time we actually fail to recognise that this is what is required for the online business side as well.

After many months of asking the questions that were important to business-leaders and entrepreneurs, as well as my own experience in the field, all the mis-beliefs, misconceptions, and mis understandings were collated to form what has been called the 7 Deadly Digital Delusions.

These are the 7 Deadly Digital Delusions that are preventing you from building your online empire.
1. Guru-speak and buzz words gets results.
2. Social Media is a strategy.
3. Online works in isolation.
4. Advertising is dead and ineffective online.
5. I don't need a "sales funnel", sales will come in time.
6. Being online is "easy", just write about a successful story.
7. Customers will always be able to find me, or, "Build it and they will come".

Why has it stopped at 7? Yes, there were many, many more. We could have made a list of the 101, or 205 of the deadliest digital delusions, however, we have encapsulated only what is really important. The ones that made the list are the most significant. These are the delusions that are most likely directly affecting your business and your business success online - the ones directly preventing you from building your online empire.

What You Can Do Next:

Each and every business may interpret these "delusions" differently. We would love to hear what you have found to be the "delusional" thought that you are experiencing. Do you want to join the discussion on the delusions that you know exist? Jot down your thoughts and ideas; the ones that you think are important to stop the misinformation and misguidance; the delusions you have encountered.

1. : _____

2. : _____

3. : _____

Do you agree with any of the 7 deadly digital delusions? Please add to this conversation by sending us your thoughts, or see what others are talking about regards their digital delusions on www.thedigitaldelusion.com/1

Why We Are Delusional

The 7 Deadly Digital Delusions presented are how we interpret what is going on in the digital world. Some may be really obvious, and others not so much. The point is that there are a number of factors that make many entrepreneurs feel powerless to what is going on; the identification of the delusions is the first step to recovery. The only way that you can build a strong business is by actually understanding where things are going a bit (or lot) off the rails, and what you need to do to overcome these issues.

These 7 Deadly Digital Delusions are intended to start the discussion on what is wrong with the current state of affairs in the industry. They are not meant to be a definitive list, but rather a dynamic list of what is possible, what can be done to stop the delusions and make a difference with businesses online.

Each of the 7 Deadly Delusions is clearly identified, followed by ways to "defeat them". Overcoming each delusion can be accomplished quite easily, as you simply need to follow the steps outlined for each stage.

In chapter 6 of this Online Empire Building Project, we further reinforce what you and your business need to accomplish to actually fully overcome these delusions, by building up your online business through the unique digital framework.

#1 Guru-speak and buzz words get results

What is it?

This is one of the fundamental delusions that everyone is subjected to. Whether it is because the majority of people don't actually understand everything that is going on, or just that there are a lot of people trying to drive into this space to become the "expert"; either can be debated, but it is in fact a combination of both.

The amount of knowledge and information that you are expected to know about being online, really is immense, and in most cases, simply overwhelming. Most businesses just want to focus on their business, not on the seemingly superfluous stuff like online marketing. It is not a sign of laziness or lack of focus either, but rather a symptom of the level of detail required to get started and stay up to date with all aspects and also implement on a regular basis. Most people will simply decide that it is not worth the trouble, and just let things fade away, hoping that it will get better "by design".

We are inundated with so much information and an array of different aspects to keep up, that it can be overwhelming for most.

From the "guru" side, many people who think that they are "entrepreneurs" feel that building up a "social media company" is quick and easy, and there will be lots of customers. It is like that old gold-rush model that doesn't really work any more. Everyone and their dog is considered a social media expert these days. You need to be able to understand what is needed, to be able to select and utilise these various services, to discover the path you need to take. You need to be able to screen people properly, to ensure that they fit with your overall messages and strategies that are at the root of your success.

The problem is not so much that more people are entering the online space, just that there is no certification, no regulation, no formal training required to get into this space. Often, the knowledge level of the so called "experts" providing the advice is sometimes questionable, and usually generated by simply surfing the web for good material. There are really very few people who can actually understand the needs of the clients aligned with the actual needs of the business.

With the volume of information always coming in, it is easier to get someone else to do the work for them. This will help you and your business, but the strategy of the actual business needs to be understood quite clearly. It needs to be clear how the different pieces fit together for your business. Every business is unique, and it does take particular skills to be able to understand and comprehend what needs to be done for an individual business and also how it needs to be done.

The word "guru" is also highly misused in this industry. In most industries or areas of expertise, it is actually a highlight of their skills and advancement to a higher level of knowledge and capabilities. In this industry however, anyone can call themselves a guru, with little or no qualifications whatsoever, further adding fuel to the fire for creating this huge chasm of misinformation.

If you are unable to complete the online development on your own, you need to source and utilise known experts in the field; people who's work you have seen directly, or those who come highly recommended. It is far too easy for anyone to put up a sign and say that they are open for business as a social media expert, or worse yet, they are part of your "target" demographic, and hence assume that they can then handle everything else, just because they are "smart about social media". It takes much, much more than this.

Anyone can sit at their computer and be a self-proclaimed Facebook expert or guru. It takes some essential business and marketing skills to be able to actually connect what is known with what is not known, and at the same time, interface and integrate what your company is specifically about and how the message is being conveyed. It's not easy being able to do this.

If you are doing the work internally, the same rules apply; you really need to get the best person for the job. They need to have the skills of strategic sensibilities, technical knowledge, and excellent means of communication.

The Reality

You would be surprised about how much you know that actually affects what you do and can do online. Online strategies come down to the essence of your business, which can be conveyed well by the business leader. Working online needs to be a close part of what you do, everyday, and needs to be integrated into everything that you do for your business. You still need to be the expert; the expert in your business. No one can do that except you.

There is also a significant amount of misinformation that is being passed around on the net, at any particular time. This goes hand in hand with the guru mentality - that they will be able to "lead you out of the woods". You can easily be overwhelmed with all of the information and expectation, as it always seems to be coming at a frightening pace. Hoping that it will simply go away or get easier, won't actually help you, as you will only be further delayed when you come up to breathe again.

Overcoming The Delusion

Every business leader's business is different. While there are principles of online work that are similar in structure, your business is unique, and the approach that you need to take in developing a strategy will also be unique. You need to be able to combine the essence of your business with an online methodology that takes into account your distinctive business.

Simply telling someone what to do is really only half the solution. You wouldn't necessarily buy half a car, or buy a house without opening the door and walking into it. While "gurus" and "experts" can be important to helping you define the basic online activity side of your strategy, understanding how your business runs is something that can only happen with a thorough understanding of it. This is how you can develop a strategy that works specifically with your business. You are the expert in your business. You need to be accountable for your business.

If you decide that you do need some external help with your business, you need to do some digging when you hire someone to complete this type of role; it is key to your business, and should be treated as such. We have created some quick questions below, which you can ask when selecting people to work with.

Keep in mind that you in fact are the "expert"; no one knows your business better than you do. It is therefore important to ensure that you fully complete the analysis as to what you need to do, in the online space. Become accountable for your business.

Tools That You Can Use

In sourcing external assistance for your online business, you need to ask and engage the person or firm fully. Don't be afraid to ask key questions that will truly point you in the direction of whether or not this person or company is for you and will help your company. You need to assess how they problem solve, and how they actually create unique strategies that will work for your business, not just off-the-shelf solutions that have been thrown in place for multiple, previous clients. It's no different than what you would do when you are interviewing someone for a job. You need to know exactly who you are getting and what they are capable of, otherwise you wouldn't hire them. You need the best people to do the best for your business.

Conduct an interview with your firm/consultant, and ask the following questions:

1. How successful are you in your own digital space?
2. Do you understand my market?
3. How connected are you to influencers in my industry?
4. What tools do you use to measure the ROI of your campaigns?
5. What are some social media campaign ideas for my business?
6. How would you handle a social media crisis?

There may not be a right answer here, however, you will quickly get to understand whether or not this person is suitable for what you want to accomplish.

A digital media consultant is essentially the eyes, ears and voice of your company online. That means you need someone who can raise your brand awareness, deliver traffic to your website, and boost your bottom line, all while keeping your company's reputation top-of-mind.

#2 Social Media and Facebook are strategies

What is it?

Many companies and individuals feel that simply having a social media strategy is all that is needed to be successful online. Or, further to that, if you have a Facebook page for your business then you are "good to go". Nothing could be further from the truth. What they are missing is the simple fact that this is only one of the things that is needed.

This delusion stems from the fact that there is much more to an online business than just one of these small elements. As we explore further, we need to have an integration of all of the different activities and strategies that make a business work better.

Often entrepreneurs believe that they just need to put up a Facebook page and everything else will fall in place. After the initial stage, you need to ask yourself - what next? How does a Facebook customer fit into your sales funnel? How do they make connections with your business? You need to be able to span across all of the different and varied parameters that are not only your business, but what your customer and audience are up to as well.

It's not just about "likes", either.

The entrepreneurs that recognise that there is a difference between Facebook and social media in general as a strategy and a tool, are then able to recognise precisely how to use this tool, and how it fits together with all of the other tools that are available to each and every business.

With the growth of social networking and social media, it is extremely important to consider that all the new avenues and channels of connecting are in fact just a tool, nothing more and nothing less. It is no different than the set of tools that you need to fix your car, or fix your house. They are usually completely different, but they are always needed.

Social media is no different. It is a tool that you can use to connect with your audience. It is, in essence, more of a "tactic" as opposed to an actual strategy. This misconception is quite frequent and almost ubiquitous, so you don't need to think that you are the only one doing this.

The challenge has always been that social media is just one piece of the overall puzzle in terms of having everything in place for your online business. There is no real magic about social media either. As we will explore in some of our online trends, it really is more about connecting what we enjoy. It is about being social.

Are there successful businesses that just use Facebook? Yes, but these are in fact quite rare. Typically, they would also be working across all of the different channels, and have implemented an integrated online strategy with all of the different components.

As more and more social media channels join the frey, keep in mind that these are all just tools in your toolbox. Sites like Myspace, once thought to be lost on the internet, has begun to make some new advancements. Google+ was also another "new" social media site that was created in 2011. You may not need these sites now. You don't need to do everything, just because you are told that it is the "next big thing". You need to analyse why it is that you would consider engaging on this level.

The Reality

Social media is a tool. Facebook is a tool. You need to be able to organise yourself appropriately, and use the tools and resources at your disposal. Everything needs to be combined together, with all of the other aspects of an online presence.

Overcoming The Delusion

Think of social media and all of the social channels as being part of your online business toolkit. You need a lot of different tools to actually build a house and being online is no different. You need to know what tool to use and when. You don't use a hammer for cutting boards to size, so likewise you should not use just one tool to build your entire online business. There are so many different tools available, that you need to be able to understand which tools best fit with your business and of course your audience. Are you a B2B or a B2C? Do you deal with "fun" type of content, sales-based, or do you work better with factual, engineering based information? These are aspects that you will need to consider in choosing what social media tools you need.

Tools That You Can Use

Look at how the different social media channels fit together, and how each one can be used for a specific task or groups of tasks. There are many choices, but you don't need to use every tool available to you in your toolbox, either.

You need to decide what is important to you and your business in assessing the channels of social media. Making a list and combining aspects of your customers and audience, in terms of where they are located, or visiting, helps you work out what is important and needs to be done.

Consider the following:

1. What channels are you currently using?
2. What channels have you considered using?
3. What channels do you feel that you must use? Why?
4. Where is your audience currently migrating? What are they using? Where are they most active? Do you have evidence of this?

#3 Online works in isolation

What is it?

Many businesses believe that what they do online is separate from what they do in their "normal" offline state. They feel that there needs to be a segregation that allows them to compartmentalise what happens within each part of their business. Further, a significant misunderstanding is that they only have to work on one specific component and are still able to get maximum results.

Businesses that are usually effective online, have already built a very strong business in their regular bricks and mortar world; in other domains. It is crucial to connect all aspects of your online business together.

The interconnection is more than just putting a Twitter handle on your business card. It needs to go much deeper than that. You need to think holistically, how the two separate parts are integrated throughout. Similar to the Online Empire Project Framework described in detail within this book, you also need to integrate everything that happens in both worlds.

Think of the Internet as being the umbilical cord that connects each "side" of your business. It connects, and more importantly, allows for your audience to reach you wherever you are, and wherever they are.

There are far too many stories of business leaders not being able to connect these two decidedly different, yet similar, aspects of their business.

Similar to one of the other delusions on this single aspect - many businesses have chosen, and wrongfully so, just to build a Facebook presence, feeling or deciding that it is all they need. Or, they can just do some SEO, or maybe run a few ads with Google. Unfortunately, this won't work, as the scope of the online world is far beyond this. Business after business fail because they are unable to connect the various aspects of a proper and thorough online business. This "connection" cannot be stressed often enough.

There are many different avenues that need to be developed for a comprehensive plan. A strong business will build a very strong foundation. As detailed in Chapter 4, there are specific components that you need to include in overcoming this delusion and building a strong foundation.

The Reality

You need to combine all of the different online avenues and channels for you, together, such as advertising, social media and SEO, among others. If you have an existing physical location, you also need to consider how to transition customers from your physical store or office locations, towards your online activities. If you choose to have a physical location, then you can easily ensure and leverage the capabilities towards compelling people online, as well as vice versa, whereby you can direct your online traffic through to your actual location.

Overcoming The Delusion

All of the components of good online best practices need to be utilised, together. Regardless of what type of business you are in, you need to have a sound strategy, a clear content plan, SEO that works, a sales or action funnel, social media, video, photographs and advertising. When planning and implementing, ensure that you follow a specific framework that allows you to capture all of the various aspects and activities along the way.

Even if you don't have a retail or food-based business, you can also push people to your physical location. This can be via mobile or activity based businesses.

It is important to engage all of the critical elements of an online strategy. These are detailed in Chapter 5, and also within the actual Online Empire Project in Chapter 6.

Fundamentally, the objective is to have both your online and offline business working in unison. You need to look at ways that you can connect your online audience with your offline store/shop or business. You can do this with such things as location redemption coupons that are displayed online, or special offers that are only accepted offline.

From your physical location, you need to engage people with such things as photo check-ins, location check-ins, or special offers and discounts to your online presence. This can also be accomplished with such things as special events where the goals and objectives are to specifically get customers or clients to move from your physical location onto your online store/shop. One of the important things to consider is properly incentivising this move from offline to online domains.

You need to engage your audience into your overall sales funnel. This then allows you to approach them at different stages of your engagement and subsequent buying cycle. The businesses that are able to engage their audience in either domain, and provide a smooth transition between the two, are the ones that will survive and become very successful. This concept will be explored further in the Online Empire Strategy.

Tools That You Can Use

To get a better idea of how your business is structured, consider the following questions:

1. Do you have an existing physical or retail location?
2. What elements of a comprehensive digital strategy do you use? SEO? Advertising? Social Media? Content Planning, etc.?
3. How can you connect your online audience with your offline activities?
4. How can you drive your audience online, from your physical locations? How do you incentivise this transaction?

#4 Advertising is dead and ineffective online

What is it?

Advertising still lives on. In fact, we will never be entirely "rid" of advertising. Similar to the paper-less office, and the "dawning of the new age of social media", when everybody would just love everything and everybody, this will not happen. Advertising will not disappear. It is integrated into society, so get used to it. You can, however, leverage it and change how you use it to actually make it successfully work for your particular business.

However, it is important to look at advertising with a different perspective. Facebook and Linkedin have begun to move or transition the types of advertising that most people will respond to. You no longer need to have some general type ad that you hope your specific target audience may or may not chance upon. It is no longer about getting just eyeballs on your ads, but rather your targeted audience. There is no longer any second-guessing; you are able to focus your advertising on specific interests, activities, passions, plus of course the regular demographics that you are used to, such as age, occupation, gender, etc. These traditional demographics, while interesting and help focus your advertisements, are not that effective. This is why "old" advertising forms do not work quite as well as the "newer" forms of advertising.

Facebook has actually moved several steps forward recently, and will no doubt continue to evolve their advertising methods, as well as the other services as they come online with specific advertising, such as Twitter, Pinterest, etc. Advertising will eventually come to all social networking services, as the services themselves also need to generate revenue.

Facebook has introduced a number of ways to connect through ads that allow you to engage with people in the Facebook network who may share similar interests. This allows you to share more information, which includes a specific post on Facebook that other people may like and share. You can even have a promoted post on images and videos that you create as part of your overall structure and framework. You are able to really interconnect your foundation throughout advertising, so that it is not linear like it used to be. You have a tremendous amount of flexibility and capabilities now, where you can directly target extremely specific audiences.

Google Adwords advertising is also the lumbering giant in terms of online advertising. More than likely have already tried to run a campaign or two on it. Maybe some of it worked, while some of it may not have worked at all, and was a large waste of money. Don't worry, as this is more common than you know.

There will always be people who complain about all forms of advertising, even if they stumbled upon it themselves, or actually used it to find a new product or service. It is engrained into how people function and operate in a consumer-based society. You need to understand who your target audience is. This will allow you to focus your advertising efforts, allowing you to "miss" those people who always complain. In more cases than not, the people who complain about your advertising, are more than likely not your customer, or are not able to actually understand how it is that you are communicating with them.

Traditional banner and interruption ads will decline however, and will be replaced by innovative offerings like Promoted Tweets and Sponsored Stories. What makes these so-called native ads unique is that they don't look like ads at all, apart from small disclaimers. They appear in-stream and read exactly like another piece of user-generated content.

While some users resent this intrusion into their home streams, these "native" ads potentially enable brands to reach clients on their own turf and on their own terms. Behind it all is the concept of convergence; the idea that ads and content can be interchangeable. This is important to understand. Companies, for instance, are already sending out Tweets to followers on their social media channels. Using analytical tools to identify which are most read, they can selectively amplify the best of the bunch as Promoted Tweets, turning content into ads and reaching an even larger audience.

The possible reason why your past or present advertising did not work as well as you had hoped or expected, was that you needed the proper foundation and framework. Advertising for the sake of advertising will not work, it needs to integrate all of the different activities across your business. This is the framework that we will be building throughout this book. There is a specific way to capture leads, sales, downloads, etc. This is part of how you set up the necessary goals for your business, and how you are offering value. These need to be integrated and compiled into your strategic sales funnel.

This book is obviously not about advertising, as that is a complete, complex subject unto itself. It is important though to understand some of the basics of advertising, and in particular the channels that are available to you and your business, in an online perspective. We won't be able to discuss traditional media advertising; this is important on a case by case basis. It should be implemented at some point. However, like online advertising, extremely specific goals and target audiences need to be set to work properly with your business.

That being said, part of the Online Empire Framework that we will build your business upon, includes advertising as part of your new strategy and revised business operations. This advertising aspect, and how it actually fits together with your entire strategy will be outlined, not just on a campaign by campaign basis. Advertising needs to be an ongoing activity - whether it is on Facebook, Linkedin, Google, or whatever other channel is appropriate to you and your business.

The Reality

Advertising is a sound strategy for creating brand awareness as well as sales and leads. Without advertising of some form, whether it is through Google adwords, mobile advertising, or social network ads/posts, you will not increase your audience and sales. Online advertising needs to be completed with specific criteria and needs to be guided and managed properly, or it can become quite pointless and expensive. Most small businesses need to allocate an appropriate amount to advertising their business activities. That being said, not all forms of advertising are "equal", especially from the perspective of aligning with your own business strategy.

Overcoming The Delusion

Currently you can develop and use highly targeted campaigns to your audience. Whether they are on Facebook or Linkedin, or just searching the web, you can usually find your audience. You need to develop campaigns that are highly focused on your target market, and utilise additional incentives, such as contests and sweepstakes. You need to be smart, however, and create a campaign that truly matches what you want your customers or audience to connect with. Test your campaigns and then adjust them as needed.

Some types of online advertising work, and some don't. You need to be very clear about your objectives - whether you are "brand building", or looking for specific sales - and then campaigns that work specifically for you and your business can be designed.

Tools That You Can Use

Ask your self these specific questions:

1. Who is your target audience? What do they like? Where do they go? What do they talk about?
2. What is your goal of advertising? Make it specific - do customers need to download something?
3. How does it fit with your sales funnel? How are you moving people towards your product/service?
4. What specifically are you actually trying to communicate with your audience?
5. What is special and unique about what you have to offer or your advertisement?
6. What is your ROI and your daily spend?
7. What channel does your audience best represent?

#5 I don't need a "sales funnel" for ROI. Sales will come in time.

What is it?

The delusion of many businesses in this area is actually quite astounding. Even today, there are numerous examples of what could best be described as a "free for all". There is no consistency to the message, and there is certainly no goal to actually move observers into leads, buyers or contacts.

It does not matter what type of business you have; you need to have a specific business goal, otherwise there is no real point. Don't lose the plot, amidst the clutter and confusion of online. The broad goal is obviously to increase or sustain revenues. The more specific goals need to be exactly what you want your audience to do. No business will grow without paying customers - even if you are a not-for-profit business, you still need to generate income to grow the business.

There are many businesses using Facebook, who seem to be just using it as a community based forum of yesteryear. There is no push towards their ecommerce site, and no mention of products that customers can buy. There simply is a collection of "nice" & "funny"... and of course cats and bacon. This does not create business; this does not inform and educate; it does not move the audience towards an eventual purchase, or even onto an email list. It is ineffective online marketing at it's finest, and something that you must avoid.

It is a seemingly simple concept, but one that is far to often overlooked. If you are unfamiliar with a sales funnel, then it is important to understand what one is. A sales funnel is all of the activities related to what you do, as a business, which drives your user or audience towards a specific goal or action. The action can be as detailed as making a purchase, or entering an email address into a sales list. You need to be able to quickly identify what it is that you are driving your audience towards, formulate that as a goal, and then push your traffic and audience towards it.

A sales funnel is not very complicated and can be fairly easy to implement. What it means, in essence, is that you have a specific goal, and a means for moving your audience and customers along the steps to reach that goal.

Your goal needs to be as simple as possible; every activity along the way then needs to direct your audience to that goal. It can be anything that is related to your business, including:

- An eBook download
- Online store purchase
- Email sign-up for a newsletter
- Contact your business for further information
- White Paper download
- Call your CSR line for information

You should consider having multiple goals as well, to fully take advantage of the behaviours surrounding each of your buying stages. This will allow your audience to be able to connect with you along different stages of the buying cycle, and also allow you to push them towards your ultimate business goal.

The Reality

Sales funnels do not necessarily imply only for a specific dollar value or "sales". A sales funnel is necessary in order to guide your audience to a conclusion or specific "action". This action can be as simple as the download of an ebook, or the completion of a form, but something needs to be in place. Sales cycles can be short or long, and it is critical that you capture your audience throughout the entire sales or activity cycle.

Overcoming The Delusion

If you operate a commerce-based site, then obviously the final action is a purchase. If you are running something less tangible, you still need to consider how to capture your audience. Even if your final action is just to inform, your site needs to be able to "capture" this step, with such things as a download, a gift, an email, entry into a contest, or something similar. When you are formulating your strategy, ensure that you understand this process and are able to add "goals" along the way.

Here is how you can establish an easy to run sales funnel for your business:

1. Set up your analytics package to include goals and other actions.

2. Always ensure there is some takeaway for your audience, at some point in the sales cycle.

3. Utilise links towards your ultimate goal, throughout all sales cycles, all channels, and all of your online and offline activities; push your audience towards your goals throughout all of these different aspects of their journey with you.

The Online Empire Framework will further help you analyse and create a sales funnel that will work with your business. The critical aspect is that you need to engage this funnel, and use it effectively.

Tools That You Can Use

Consider these questions in analysing your sales funnel:

1. What are the top 3 goals that you want your audience to "take-away"?

2. What does your sales funnel look like?

3. How will you connect these goals to your actual website?

4. When will you implement your revised sales funnel?

5. How will you monitor and engage your audience along your sales funnel?

What is it?

"All I need to do is put up a website, and it will be like opening up a new bank account that is never empty" - wrong. One of the biggest delusions is that the web is somehow some magical rags to riches type scenario. The ongoing and never-ending gold rush of the 21st century. The Internet is just awash in money to be made for everyone...

You have probably seen those dreadful ads, where unscrupulous businesses are touting, "as a mum, I just made $13,421 online, and now I can show you how". It's difficult to cut through all of this, as the lizard brains are wired to try to be the ultimate opportunist, and truly believe that we can live off the avails of simple work.

Even if you have a "legitimate" business, you need to be aware that the journey of taking it from your idea to an online empire, is going to take time, and it is going to take resources, and of course, it is going to take money.

You can add to this that it is most certainly not going to be easy.

For some reason, and perhaps because of the "Internet riches" mentality, a lot of businesses believe that it is a very easy task to do, and that once your business is set up, it just is a matter of letting it run on autopilot. Nothing could be further from the truth.

The average business only spends a fraction of the available resources directed towards online activities, when in fact; they need to spend additional resources. However, they need to be smart about it. They need to treat online like it is extremely important for their business, which of course, it is. Companies are not focusing on the online domain of their business because they simply do not understand what they 'should' be doing online.

The Internet has always been spoken of as the greatest opportunity our generation has ever seen. The reality is slightly different though, as many are not actually taking full advantage of this. A typical business will usually spend only around 10% of its time and resources for it's online component. Can you imagine how big the industry could become, if we even spent a little more of our resources here? This can be a competitive advantage by addressing this huge chasm between what is available and what businesses are actually doing.

As the Business Leader, you need to dedicate the necessary resources; you need to commit to getting the job done. If you really want to engage the process and begin to build your business breakthrough, then you need to use the Online Empire Framework - this will help you sort through what is important so that you can actually dedicate and focus all of your activities appropriately.

Dedication to your online business means that you have to commit to it at the same level as you would for sales and general marketing; you simply can't relegate your online domain to "when you get around to it". Every day you need to work it, like a business, or it will simply not work.

The Reality

Online takes significant work and dedication, yet often, many businesses do not apply all of the necessary resources that could be used to make it work. Your story is important, but it also is the implementation that makes the biggest difference. It takes work and it takes resources. You need to either do the online work yourself, or assign the activities. It takes commitment as a business leader.

Overcoming The Delusion

While you need to tell your story, you also actually need to "work it". Many businesses talk about blogging, yet never actually do it. You need to have a clear schedule that allows you to prioritise all of your content, ideas and topics. Then you need to get down to business and actually put it in action. Consider activities such as blogging as core to your business - if you don't do it regularly, your business will fail. It is as important as having sales people on the floor of your traditional store. You also need to ensure that you complement all of your online activity together, including press releases, cross promoting your feeds, all with the ultimate goal of building your community online. Press releases are a good way to allow others to find and connect with you, not just used to get your story out there.

Tools That You Can Use

Here is what you can do, to work 'on' your business:

1. Dedicate 30-40% of your time as a minimum to the online domain of your business. This includes daily writing and developing your sales funnel.

2. Understand and schedule your daily activities based on your online activities as a priority.

3. Consider how you will schedule your staff towards alignment of your strategy and your business' daily working activities.

4. What key tasks need to be accomplished by you and your staff to "work" your business?

5. What new goals can you set towards building your online empire, in terms of budgets, staff resources?

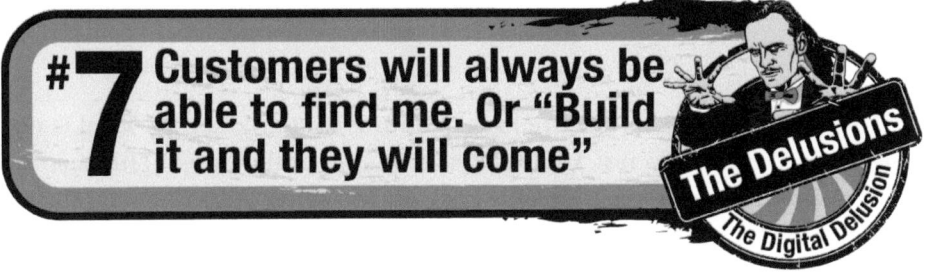

What Is It?

We have all heard the expression - build it and they will come. This is the lazy man (and women's) guide to making things happen. The truth is, and not surprisingly, is that it just does not work like that.

We have all heard it before; the Internet is an extremely complicated "web" of connections and terms, images and files. It is almost never ending. There are 571 websites created online every single minute of every day, and 48 hours of video are uploaded to Youtube in the same amount of time. If you are not doing the right things at the right time, then no one will find you.

In the "old" days, you could set up a shop in your local town or city, put up a sign, stock your shelves, and people would be able to find you, as the journey was not usually that complicated, and your business was typically the only one, or one of a few out there. That scenario no longer exists. With the global market that is now opened up in front of you through the net, the level of competitors has increased, and at the same or a greater level to your own business. Today, you simply will not stand out amongst the clutter online; it is just too big to overcome on your own.

This book outlines a number of different activities that you need to complete on a regular basis in order to get found. It is not just about SEO, or Search Engine Optimisation. Everything you do online can be searched, and indexed by the search engines - not just the text of your website, but also the images, photos, videos, and any other type of media that you can imagine. There are a number of activities that need to be integrated across your new online empire strategy that will make it easier to get found online. Without them, and without a sound strategy, you will simply not be found online, other than from friends and family, and maybe only if they feel sorry for you.

On the other side of this argument is of course viral marketing. Viral is not a strategy. We are also not talking about "going viral", either. This term is really something non-existent, and is similar to tying your financial future on winning the next Powerball lottery. If this is your strategy, then you are more than likely not going to survive.

Common sense says that "viral-ness" of something is not something that you can go to the bank on. If something does go viral, then consider it a bonus; you need to have a complete and effective strategy in place though, prior to this happening, otherwise you will not be able to capitalise on it. "Viral" is almost no different than the definition of a "fad", whereby it is very unique, but it is also very brief. Nothing can really prepare you for viral marketing - it is far more productive to build an online empire that is based on more advanced consistent strategies, rather than a reptilian response to business and markets through viral marketing.

Part of the problems in this area is also the so-called "magic pill" scenario with SEO – search engine optimisation. Unfortunately this is a very difficult area to work in. What this means is that many SEO Professionals will try to sell you a strategy that is designed to "Get you listed as #1 on Google". While this may be a reasonable goal, it is often misguided. What search terms will people be looking for you? Are people going to click on you more because of this? What other channels can you be located on? This approach to SEO is very one-dimensional, and doesn't take into consideration all of the cornerstones of a complete and sound online strategy. The online empire framework will create the structure you need in all avenues of your COMPLETE online strategy and implementation.

The Online Empire Project is based more on "Organic" SEO, meaning SEO that you can build naturally in your complete online presence. This means simple things like always fully describing you and your business in every channel that you operate in, writing PR across the Internet, blogging at least once a week, changing the content on your website, etc. These are all activities that are outlined within the Framework.

The Reality

Instant traffic generators do not exist. While it is easy to just "run some ads" to build traffic, you also have to have a sound foundation to be able to manage and actually utilise the online advertising that you do use. Further, while Google and the other search engines will eventually find you, this will take some time and effort on your part. Similar to online being "easy", there is significant amount of involvement and engagement that must happen for you to build your audience and community. Building a website or putting together a Facebook fan page, will not generate traffic into your sales funnel unless you take an active role in it.

Overcoming The Delusion

When you are planning, building and executing your website, ensure you build into your framework a follow-on plan that allows you to engage on all levels. You also need to constantly supply your website and all of your social channels with progressive, engaging and interactive content on all levels. Look at your sales funnel and find out where the attraction points are - then isolate these with your specific content and channel strategies. Consider how you look at SEO from a holistic perspective - you do need to understand the basics of what is important here, and how these will actually be able to help your business site.

Tools That You Can Use

Here are some questions to ask yourself, as you build your online empire:

1. Are you using "formal" SEO? If so, what are the specific goals that you have set out?

2. What other activities are you engaged in to bring traffic to your "goals"? PR, Blog, advertising?

3. How often do you write PR or your blog? Is this a weekly activity or whenever you get around to it?

4. How are people finding you now? From where are they finding you? Content based or activity based?

Defeating the Digital Delusions

Once you understand the digital delusions, you can then be guided towards building a complete and comprehensive solution for your business. You know a lot more about your business, and hopefully we have instilled some additional confidence in what you can do, and more importantly, what you now know online.

The Online Empire Building Project is the framework that will be developed in Chapter 6. It allows you to actually put what you now know to good use and practice. The framework allows you to quickly and easily assess what you need to do and how you need to do it, to avoid past, current, and future digital delusions.

Here's where it gets easy, at least intellectually. Embedded within the 7 Frames Online Empire Framework, are in fact the solutions to all of the 7 Deadly Digital Delusions. Each step along the way of the new framework answers all the queries and unknowns associated with them. This is how you overcome the delusions. The Framework allows you to integrate, across all areas of your business, the tools and strategy needed to build your online business breakthrough; to find your point of success, online.

You need to embrace what is going on, so that you can continue to stay on top of things. You are not required to you become an expert in everything, as that is simply not realistic; you need to ask the questions that get the answers that are important for you and your business. Become accountable to your own business.

The 7 Deadly Digital Delusions presented are how we interpret what is going on in the digital world. Some may be really obvious, and others not so much. There are a number of factors that make us feel powerless to what is going on. The only way to build a strong business is by actually understanding where things are going a bit off the rails, and what you need to do to overcome that.

When the 7 Deadly Delusions was first drafted, I quickly had a list that expanded into the dozens. This list had to be reduced to something manageable and effective that could be worked with. Some of the key areas that are important to all online businesses were highlighted, and placed into a final list of what is important. We then distilled what was the most important so that you can then focus on what is important for your business.

The 7 Deadly Delusions were intended to start the discussion on what is wrong with the current state of affairs in the industry. They are not meant to be a definitive list, but rather a dynamic list of what is possible, what can be done to stop the delusions and make a difference with businesses online.

Now that the 7 most important deadly digital delusions have been presented, we want to get your opinion.

Do you agree? Are we completely wrong?

Please list three of these digital delusions that you have encountered, that you know or think could be affecting how you work online. Are they dangerous? Do you suspect that they could grow quite bigger if you let them? Will they affect you further?

My Digital Delusion #1: _____

My Digital Delusion #2: _____

My Digital Delusion #3: _____

What other digital delusions have you encountered?

1. What is the delusion?
2. How can you identify it?
3. How can you defeat it?

"The nation's first home computer service, which brought customers computer services by telephone, is going out of business after 6 months because people don't trust computers."
   - Williamson Daily News, 1973

Discover more details of the digital delusions and how you can overcome them.

Scan QR Code or Link here: www.thedigitaldelusion.com/1

"Who the hell wants to hear actors talk?"

- HM Warner, founder of Warner Brothers, 1927

What You Need To Know

This chapter defines the emotions behind online work, how to develop a better connection through emotions, and how to make this work for your business.

You will learn:

1. Where IS the "emotion" online?
2. How to make connections online.
3. How to shut down the constant barrage of information.

Getting to Therapy

Therapy is a marvellous word. We can all use more of it. It helps us recognise that we actually have a problem and we are doing something about it; that we need help. We all do. Trust us.

We need help getting our heads around what IS "digital", as well as the emotions that motivate everyone throughout all online (and offline) experiences. Why? Because it will help you target in on what is the true motivating force for your customers, and the corollary to that, is that you will be able to interact and engage better if you actually understand what your customers need and want.

There is a lot of psychology attached to buying. We aren't here to teach you the mechanics and theories of what works and what doesn't - we are here to provide an outline to some of the key questions that you need to know the answers to, that will help you capture your audience, online.

There are numerous emotions accessible to us in the online domain. The digital domain really is lacking a lot of aspects. One of the significant things is all about LOVE. Yes, the real love. Why does this really matter? Well, people will do some amazing things when they "love" you. Think about it for a moment; if someone loves you, or if someone just thinks of you as a friend, there really is a huge difference in what the meaning of that relationship is about. The online domain, is in essence, no different. The problem stems from the fact that it is really hard to convey love, online, as there are so many barriers, and no connection in most cases. So, you land out with a bunch of "friends" who are not really engaging you, or picking up the dirty laundry for you. To engage fully, you need more of that love potion. This will be part of our therapy for you.

The second key aspect of this therapy program is a digital detox. Just as in the real domain it is necessary for a toxic cleanse every now and then, so to is it in the digital domain. We get inundated with considerable information. Being connected for so long and through so many modes, means that you can become overwhelmed, or get so self-absorbed that you are not able to actually get things done, or feel very confused about things. There can be a negative reaction, where you try to shut down, but that can also leave too many unanswered ideas and concepts wavering in the wind. The digital detox is something you need to do, once you set upon the steps of building your online empire project. Why? You will be able to actually focus on the empire building, and leave the reptilian and monkey brains back where they belong. These are the parts of your brain that keep you stranded and captive on the day to day "island", where you can't get any traction. It is messy, and very confusing.

These concepts may seem quite dichotomous. You may be asking - you want us to love everything, yet at the same time, take out the emotion so that we can actually detoxify? This is exactly the point. These two aspects are not mutually exclusive - you need to understand that you need some "love online" to engage your audience, but you also need to remove some of your monkey brain tactics that are jeopardising your online empire futures.

How do you calculate an ROI on love? Think about that when you are asking to calculate the ROI of social media. You can count how many dates you have, how many dinners you went out on, how many kisses; yet, you cannot say who you are with, or why you are no longer with your partner. You can't put a score on love online, either.

Online Customer Love

Lovemarks is a marketing concept that is intended to supposedly replace the "idea" of brands. This idea was first widely publicised in a book of the same name written by Kevin Roberts, CEO of the advertising agency Saatchi & Saatchi. Roberts claims that "Brands are running out of juice"(Roberts, 2006). He states quite simply that love is what is needed to rescue brands from mediocrity (Roberts, 2006). Without love, what exactly do you have?

Having personally seen Roberts present this concept at its infancy in 2006, it was a touchstone point for embodying emotion online, and further developing online businesses, and connecting with the audience. Maybe something about emotional intelligence here and how leading businessmen have this?? Daniel Goleman material is good

Online Love & The Digital Detox

The questions that need to be asked are, "What builds loyalty that goes beyond reason? What makes a truly great love stand out?". Roberts (2006) suggests that there are some key ingredients needed to create and sustain lovemarks. A Lovemark's "High Love" is infused with these three intangible, yet very real, ingredients: Mystery, Sensuality and Intimacy (Roberts, 2006).

- "Mystery" draws together stories, metaphors, dreams and symbols. It is where past, present and the future become a single unit. Mystery adds to the complexity of relationships and experiences because people are drawn to what they don't know. If we knew everything, there would be nothing left to learn or to wonder at, right? If any of the above is Robert's ideas, you would need to reference it. Same for below

- "Sensuality" keeps the five senses on constant alert for new textures, intriguing scents and tastes, wonderful music; sight, hearing, smell, touch, taste. Our senses work together to alert us, lift us, and transport us. When they are stimulated at the same time, the results are unforgettable. It is through the five senses we experience the world and create our memories.

- "Intimacy" means empathy, commitment and passion. The close connections that win intense loyalty as well as the small perfect gesture. These are often remembered long after functions and benefits have faded away. Without intimacy people cannot feel they own a brand, and without that conviction, a brand can never become a Lovemark.

Roberts (2006) explains the relationship between lovemarks and other selling concepts through a simple schema

How Can Your Audience Fall in Love With You, Online?

based on respect and love. The full schema is as follows: mere products (commodities) command neither love nor respect. Fads attract love, but without respect, this love is just a passing infatuation. Brands attract respect, even lasting respect, but without love. Lovemarks, explains Roberts (2006), command both respect and love. This is achieved through the trinity of mystery, sensuality, and intimacy.

These are truly intriguing concepts. The background as such really allows us to think about our own perspectives, and how we are really making a difference. As we "evolve" online, we are going to need to further develop this aspect; we can no longer afford to be just about a purchase here or a download there. We really need to connect fully with our audience. As you embark upon your Online Empire Project, you will need to bring your emotions forward. You will need to bring the love of your products and brands to the forefront.

Is this just marketing drivel, or is there something behind all of this? During the research phase of this book, it was believed that the only way to create real interest was through an up swell of emotion directed to your audience. Could this be "love"? We're not exactly sure either, just that we felt we would be much further ahead if we could create a deeper connection.

The fact remains, however, that fundamentally, the reason that people will either chose you or not, is in essence more about the emotions that they feel during the lead up to the point of purchase. If they don't feel any emotion, then they probably won't purchase, unless it is simply a commodity. That being said, have you ever watched people purchase seemingly basic items like fruits and vegetables? Most people really want to pick up the food item and try to connect with it to see if it is worthy to purchase? Is this love? Maybe not, but there is an emotion that can be explored here.

You need to connect with your audience, not just from the technical, electronic aspect, but from the emotional connection between the feelings of your products and what you are developing with you customer. Therefore, you need to create an emotional connection with your products or services.

There are many examples of brand "love", or absolutely raving, fanatical fans, online. They are seen online regularly. These include sites that get a tremendous amount of traffic, like Apple, Redbull and Coke or Facebook pages that have millions of fans. The difference between successful work online is that you have and need to create engagement. An engaged audience is an audience that is more in love with you than others. You don't have to have a million fans to really connect with your audience; it is not just about that. You do need to develop the connections, typically through finding the core loves of your audience, and reflecting that in your products, platforms and your own marketing. It can be a fair struggle at the beginning, but it is important to consider what emotions are driving your audience as they engage you and make purchases. Alternatively, what emotion are you perhaps mistakenly exhibiting that may be pushing your customers away? It is no different than finding a perfect, personal match.

Currently, there is little or no emotion in online domains. This really exacerbates the situation, and YOU need to change this. So how do you create emotional connections throughout this process, to elevate your business above others? What if you were able to embody emotion into your online domains, when nobody else is? You would be far beyond what your competitors are doing. Consider implementing the three principles of Lovemarks, of Mystery, Sensuality & Intimacy, as you embark upon your Online Empire Project.

Questions to contemplate to add more "love" to your business, and connect on more of an emotional level:

1. What fundamental emotion can you convey in your business?

2. In the past, what have people responded to directly, with regards your business?

3. What has your audience NOT responded to?

4. Have you ever asked your audience what they really like or "love" about your product? What have they said?

5. If you could create an emotional connection with your audience, what would it be?

The Digital Detox

The amount of information (and misinformation) that entrepreneurs are subjected to is immense. It can be very overwhelming. Whether just trying to ascertain a quick fact, or working entirely digitally, everyone is seemingly pressed to their limits in terms of what they are exposed to; a constant, never-ending amount of information.

The Detox is more about controlling the reptile responses and the monkey moments, it allows focus on the empire building brain.

A lot of times escaping from it all seems like the path to take. Perhaps being a hermit isn't such a bad idea, anymore? But how do we go about doing this?

As a business leader, you simply can't, but you can reduce these streams of information; you can detoxify your system as much as possible, to get the maximum value out of what you do online.

Distractions are huge, online. Often we are looking at, or for, something quite specific online, then suddenly looking at photos, videos, checking email, or worse yet, checking Facebook or Twitter to see what is going on, just happens. How often do you sit on Facebook, waiting for the news feed to change... There is that constant anticipation that something "new" is about to happen very, very soon. The original distraction may have been email, where yes, checking and refreshing constantly, or quickly rushing into the email program when "that" tone or beep from the computer is heard, happens. These distractions are constant; and they are very prevalent in everything.

The Digital Detox runs deep into the whole Empire Building concept. It is one of the core reasons for actually embarking upon this journey, as a lot of what is said and done online, is part of the clutter of information. We are the creators and perpetrators of this clutter, as well as what we cause audiences to endure. Keep in mind that it is not a therapy session - you'll need to get that elsewhere.

Some of the basic problems and mistakes of being online are actually directly related to this inundation of information. Relevance to you and your audience is key here. A certain level of relevance needs to be created by you. If you build a website, do you 'exist'?; the clear answer is 'no', as you have no relevance to what you are and what you do.

You simply do not 'exist' online. No one knows you. No one cares. You are irrelevant and invisible. You are obscure amongst the mountains of information and online "stuff" that is already out there. You are not competing just against your own industry competitors either, in this global Internet - you are also competing against every single business around the world that is targeting the exact same customer. Guess what? Clients are simply not finding you, and you are becoming more and more irrelevant online.

This Digital Detox is intended for you, as a business leader building a business online, as well as for your audience, whom, in essence, has experienced a similar level of being overwhelmed, digitally. The digital detox is meant to increase and develop your relevance and presence, by actually reducing the amount of clutter that you and your business perpetuates. Call it "responsible posting"; something that allows for everyone to benefit from - both from the reader's perspective, as well as from the businesses'.

Part of the overall strategy of the 7 Frames Online Empire Project is to actually create that needed relevance, as well as the framework that you will be able to build and use, to guide your audience and customers towards your online goals and actions. There is no other way to do this - without a framework, you will continue to remain irrelevant, as nothing is connected; your audience can see this, even more than you.

Once a customer actually finds that one link, story or photo that caught their eye and caused the click, what do they do next? They have landed on your website and... they leave - almost as quickly as they entered, and are never to be seen again, as you have not shown any relevance, no actions, no goals. By creating the integrated framework of the 7 Frames Online Empire Project, the necessary infrastructure will be in place for you to get your customer to move towards your online goals. You become relevant, and you can then your audience to subsequent stages of your sales funnel and sales cycle.

Other connections to the Digital Detox will be discussed later on in the book, including the whole concept of "editing" what is seen and done online.

So, the critical question is, how exactly do we complete a "Digital Detox"? How do we shut things down so that we can actually undertake something useful? Perhaps that is why some businesses don't actually enjoy being online, as they see it as a real threat to becoming even more distracted, with even less time to work with building their business.

The Detox really is more about the amount of information that you are confronting, and continuing to put online. Cut down what you feel you need to distribute, by planning a clear outline, you can cut down what needs to be distributed to your audience. Do you have a content plan? This is a critical step, is needed and part of this book. It will allow you to be clear on what messaging you are trying to convey, and how you plan to do it. There is no need to continue to clutter what is going on. Many are already having too much trouble finding you online as it is. If you are on message, and on target with your customer and audience, you will be able to generate and increase your relevance.

Relevance, as explained, is absolutely critical for sustaining and building your online audience. There is no second place for relevance. Either you are, and people are finding you, or you are not, and no one could care less. There is no in-between; it is definite.

There are two keys that you need to remember; you are in it for yourself and your business, but also for your audience and your customer. These are both different scenarios, and while they need to be dealt with differently, they share some commonality also, and they are not mutually exclusive.

To summarise, this is what you need to think about in order to help reduce your clutter in the Internet ecosystem:

1. Develop a clear strategy - know the exact reasons why you are online, and what you are trying to do.
2. Reduce the clutter - don't post for the sake of posting; clear messaging is critical at all times (develop a content plan).

3. Feed into the sales funnel. Shorten the buying cycle by ensuring that purchase information is available from many, different angles.

4. Set Goals - determine exactly what you want to achieve, and what you want your audience and customer to "do" or "complete".

The key ingredient is to ensure that you always prioritise your messaging - both the incoming and the outgoing. A sound strategy and content plan helps you with the outgoing. If you want to take on a more proactive approach to your own use of online channels, for a "personal" digital detox, try these tactics:

1. Unplug when you are working; building that prezo or spreadsheet, or writing your blog (hint, hint)? Close your browser.

2. Check your email only at specific intervals; maybe every 2-3 hours.

3. Put your mobile phon0 away for a while.

4. When you are plugged in, control the amount of time you spend on your social channels for work and pleasure. While sometimes distractions are fine, you need to control your own time spent, which can turn into unproductive time.

Now, identify your customer and customer journey, to help you reduce your clutter. Questions to develop and consider:

1. Who is your audience/customer?

2. What things are they interested in?

3. Where do they go, online - for fun, for business, for purchasing?

4. What do they buy, how do they buy it?

5. How do you measure relevance? How do you think you can measure it?

6. Do you always have a clear purpose when you post online?

Want to get a "Digital Detox Certificate", and how to find out how you are can further reduce clutter online for yourself and everyone else?

www.TheDigitalDelusion.com

> "I predict the internet... will soon go spectacularly supernova and in 1996, catastrophically collapse."
>
> - Robert Metcalfe, Ethernet Inventor, 1996

Delusional?

Discover what love can mean to your brand, online.

Scan QR Code or Link here: www.thedigitaldelusion.com/1

CHAPTER 5: Digital Trends Shaping Your Business
The Digital Delusion

"Man will not fly for 50 years."

- Wilbur Wright in 1901

What You Need To Know

This chapter is about understanding the trends and factors that are affecting the online industry in general.

You will learn:

1. How to identify some of the trends that are affecting your business.//
2. How to leverage these trends to assist with your business.
3. About specific elements required to help build your online empire.

Dominant Trends For Online Businesses

Trends help organise information into segments that you can then create relations with. There is a specific science that can analyse trends; there are trend experts that can also attempt to predict what trends are common and will continue to grow in size and in reach. Predicting trends is not very easy, and of course fraught with all kinds of errors and inconsistencies. Don't worry though - you don't need to be a trend expert; you just need to be able to understand the underlying factors that are the foundation of the interactions that are your business, and of course driven by your customer needs.

Trends are not like a crystal ball - they don't predict nor tell the future. They are not mystical or have super powers. What they do is delineate a key "pattern" or behaviour that is being exhibited by a large group of people over a long period of time.

You have probably heard of the terms trend watching or trend hunting; this is the so-called identification of "trends", or in most cases, just capturing the weird and odd, but sometimes quite isolated consumer behaviours. These identifiers don't really or necessarily identify a trend per se, just something different that someone happens to have noticed. You don't need to become a trend watch or trend seeker to make a proper assessment of what is going on in your business and industry, you just need to have a broad idea of what exactly is driving or sustaining your business.

Why are trends important? They primarily create a foundation or reference point. This then allows businesses to understand whether or not what they are building will last a long time, or not (i.e. a fad). Building a long-term business on a shorter-term trend is possible, you just need to have a serious exit plan in place. The best way to grow a business however is to build it upon a longer-term trend; more value is obviously associated if it is the start of a very strong trend, such as Facebook and online social networking.

How do you know if a trend is growing, maintaining or reducing? There are several key indictors that can help point you in the right direction:

1. Are there more competitors entering into the industry?

2. Are consumers/customers asking for something very specific that may not be part of the current market offering?
3. Is the price of the product/service rising or falling?

It is important that you develop an understanding for the trends that are driving the online domains, but more importantly, your business. Analyse what trends are present in your industry, so that you can better navigate and capitalise on them. You don't have to become trend watchers; just understand what your audience is thinking.

What trends are at the base of the overall online business domains? There are primarily three that illustrate what we are doing, how we are doing it, and what it means. These trends help create the associations to building your business. Yes, these affect you and what you do.

The trends that seem quite strong and are influencing what is said and done online are guided by three core concepts. They are the essence of what is happening in and around the online world of business. They capture that underlying reason why things are happening in a particular way.

Every person is different, yet they all seem to be engaged by three simple principles: Connecting, Telling, and Editing. These three aspects are what is tying everyone "together".

The three new touchstones of online consumerism are:

CONNECTING TELLING EDITING

How do we put these building blocks together in a world that sometimes seems overwhelming? What do we do when we become overwhelmed? What if we could break this down into what we can clearly see is happening and developing throughout our never-stop world of advertising, communication, personal space, personal and management?

Understanding your principle trends will help you grow your business and anticipate your future.

Everyone does this, whether they consciously decide to or not. It is as simple as observing what others do on a daily basis, how they process information, what they are about, and how they interact and connect with the world. This idea is nothing new, other than the way that we can actually view these insights by organising and articulating them in this manner. We have all seen it before, but sometimes we have trouble actually being able to interpret the many things that surround us.

You need to find out how consumers are further shaping their online world through "telling" about themselves on Facebook, Twitter, or the myriad of social networking; "connecting" their world with technology and mobile devices, and finally, how they "edit" all of this information into useful, sizable chunks that can then be managed and acted upon.

How do you, as a marketer and entrepreneur navigate this and enable your company for more effective understanding of your consumer? The first part is simply understanding what is going on in their world.

Ask yourself these questions:

1. What trends do you feel are affecting your business?
2. How did you identify these trends?
3. What trends specific to your industry can cause your business to decrease?
4. What can you do to identify new trends that can be capitalised on; trends that lead to opportunities, for you and your business?
5. Think big - what future trends do you believe you will see? Relate these to your actual business. How does this possibility affect your outcome and current strategy?

Telling

Most people want to be famous or want their so-called 15 minutes of fame. However, nowadays people want more than 15 minutes. "I am Famous" is at the heart of everything we do. Some people may consider it narcissism, but it really is a simple form of human expression. Some people are just more inclined to do more.

"Telling" is at the core of how we express ourselves, and how we feel important about ourselves and within our social groups. If humans were not considered a social animal, then this would not be a key component of how we create these interactions. We are social, so we need to deal with it. With all of the social media channels, they are in fact the ultimate form of personal expression, along with the ability to "tell" or rather in the current vernacular, "share". "Telling" allows us to inform everyone of what we are doing and thinking, and why it is important to ourselves. It constantly and instantly "tells" about our personality, thoughts and beliefs.

You have seen "telling" firsthand online. People really enjoy talking about themselves. About 40% of everyday speech is devoted to telling others about what we feel or think. It is even more prevalent now, that the medium has changed so much, to where anyone who can "talk" will certainly "tell".

Where does this come from? Well, as previously mentioned, it is all about the moment of fame, brought to light more so in the last 5-10 years. "I am famous" is about telling the world that you are important, and even more important than everyone else. This is one's moment of truth, so to speak

You can quickly see that being famous is the goal, or even expectation of practically everyone. Even people who do not post regularly online, are very interested to see what other people are saying, or rather thinking. You want them to think of you. We want confirmation, we want to feel special, and we want people to see that we are better and more interesting than others. We are all after attention, whether we believe it or not. Yes, this is our ego. Social media has a disproportionate amount of ego online.

Why is this important? How do you make this work for your business? If you are able to build a relevant business, and if you create a strong following, then the people who are actually following you, your audience, will then be "telling" about you and what you do. This doesn't come easy though, as stated before. It takes a significant amount of effort to truly build a strong, thriving community. But, when you do, once everything has clicked into place, then your audience becomes your medium for spreading more about what you do, how you help them out, and how you solve their problems.

You do, however, need to have a proper framework in place so that once others are willing and able to talk about you, then you have the platform and capabilities to make it extremely easy to facilitate this. This is "true" sharing;

1. Wanting to share,
2. Having something to share, and
3. Having the necessary tools and platform to be able to share.

The framework created as part of this book, can actually be quite easy to establish and set-up. The important thing is that you actually have one. You have to think about how everything that surrounds the essence of your business, can be shared with others with absolutely little to no effort. This is where you can take this trend and make it work for your business. This is what we discuss in the social and sharing section of the Online Empire Project.

Questions to ask yourself:

1. What do you talk about, when you have nothing to talk about? Something to talk about?
2. What does your customer talk about?
3. How do you "expose" people's egos to help you spread your message?
4. What tools do you have in place for people to share everything that is yours?
5. How much of your content is currently shared? How can you "help" them share more?

Connecting

You've obviously heard of the statement that "everyone and everything is connected". This is nothing new. What is new is the way in which it is embodied and integrated into everything that we do. You are no longer considered connected, if you only have an email address and an internet connection. Today, it is about mobile access that is ubiquitous.

Unless you have a smartphone, you are no longer part of a contributing member of society.

While connecting is about having a mobile or personal device, it is also about how everything else is connected, or rather interconnected - this is more what this trend is about. It is about integration, or even homogenization. All the different nodes of our life have been integrated across our own personal spectrum, and then further across all of our links. Six Degrees of Separation (or Six Degrees of Kevin Bacon, as some of us prefer) are no longer six - we have reduced this, because of our inter-connectedness, to 3.43 (Bakhshandeh, 2011).

Just for fun. Enter 'Bacon Number' in Google, along with an actors name, and Google will provide the actual Kevin Bacon Number.

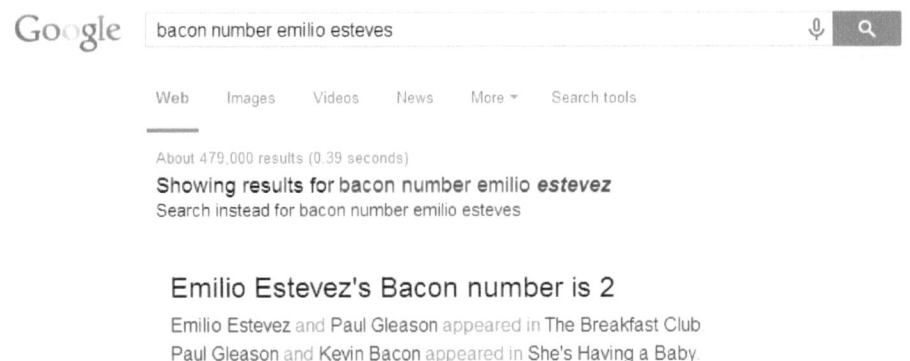

It is clear that connecting is not only about the devices that inhabit our lives, but also for the human inherent desire to be in contact with others. It is a way for people to actually utilise technology to connect in that psycho-social manner. It is not just about mobile/smart phones, they are just a tool; it is more about establishing relationships with others, connecting with everyone and everything. In other words, the act of connecting is accomplished by technology; the reason for connecting is established by the human psyche. Everything is about how we connect with fellow humans, who allow us to understand what our businesses need to do, and where they need to be doing it.

You can create some truly amazing connections with your audience and customers, as many are already interconnected in multiple levels.

What happens when we are connected by "1"; when we have reached that point of maximum communication, where everyone "knows" everyone; or rather, every one is inherently connected to each and every other person. Is this possible?

Think of the variety of tools that are used everyday to connect with each other, whether decisively active, or more passive in interactions. Here are some of the communication tools that are used to connect with one another.

1. Smart phones
2. Mobile phones
3. Laptops
4. PC's
5. Tablets
6. ATMs
7. Mobile displays
8. Billboards
9. Shopping Centre Info Kiosks
10. Text Message
11. DVD Rental Machines

Why does this trend relate to what you are doing as a business? You need to establish these various points or nodes of connections. Are you going to utilise mobile, or are you more about building a local presence with such things as QR codes, RFID. You need to be able to properly identify the connection nodes that your customers and audience are active on, and also the ones that they are not so active on. You can then understand what you need to be able to interact effectively with them.

So how do you find this out? You can, quite simply ask them; you can also use analytics to measure this; or just watch for specific behaviours - are they responding to something that is only accessible on their connecting devices, such as text messaging? Analytics will tell you exactly how people are viewing your information, whether it is from a tablet, a phone, or their PC. Information is everywhere; it just needs to be extracted.

This is where analytics comes into play, and is part of the 7 Step Online Empire Project. You can establish where your audience is, and how they are connecting. Utilising tools and analytics can give you that exact information. Then, you can continue to build your relevance and knowledge base by working with your customers, where they are.

More questions to ask yourself:

1. After mapping out your day, what devices do you use throughout the day, to keep you in connection with others? How does your customer "connect"?

2. What happens when you "drop out"? What are you missing out on?

3. What happens to you when the power goes out, the network goes down, or you can't get your proper mobile phone coverage? Do you panic? See the chapter on detox if you do!

Editing

Society today is inundated with too much information. Not just in terms of the quantity of the information, but also the quality. The amount of information and "stuff" around is really overwhelming.

You are not alone. No where is this more predominant than in the online world. It is hard to turn off, or decompress from everything that is out there. Due to this inundation of information, you need to be extremely selective and precise as to what you want to see, and what you just get in a casual glance. Yes, you may miss things, and of course forget things, but the important thing is that you need to edit the information quickly so that you can maintain some semblance of being "whelmed".

The reticular activator – the part of your brain that cognitively notices things - is working overtime with online businesses. People are constantly trying to cut down on what they are seeing, and what they are engaging. Don't worry - it's normal that you don't pick up on everything that you see.

We are bombarded with billions of bits of information, everyday. Our brains would literally shut down in midstream if we were not able to fully "edit" all incoming information. This information comes from everywhere, and it is overwhelming most of the time, so we simply shut it out.

Well, it is all a function of the brain, trying to cut down on all of the surrounding stimulus. Your brain, up until that point, simply chose to ignore 'that' information. Can you imagine what would happen if we actually were able to receive and comprehend every little detail? It would literally blow our mind.

Being online is actually no different. As you are already aware, we are constantly bombarded and inundated with masses and masses of information. Do you recall the digital detox that was mentioned previously? Well, there was a reason for this, both for you and your business - and more importantly for your customers and audience.

We edit and continue to edit, down to specific things that relate to us, or more importantly, things that create immediate understanding and relevance. Relevance, while it may be somewhat of a buzzword, and part of our delusional mindset, is actually much more than just a buzzword.

Relevance is not only what our own brains are seeking to understand in order to edit, but it is also how all of the search engines actually populate search results. Think of it this way, when you type in "summer cafe in bondi", the search engines are trying very precisely to find out what is relevant to your search, and then create a number of "suggestions" for you to find out if they interest you. Google is gambling with this, but it is trying to determine the ultimate goal of understanding the reason for your search, and hence the relevance of it to you. This is of course going on a billion times a second, as Google searches for relevance.

While we are editing within our minds, we are editing down to relevance. This is critical for two primary aspects. The first is for your audience, so that they can connect with you quickly, as they have activated their reticular activator. In order for this to happen, you need to connect with your content, which leads us to the second aspect - being able to create content that is prolific and pervasive, so it constantly creates the triggers for our brain to activate. Think of it like consistency in logos, and consistency in topics.

Google has outlined some aspects of this with their ZMOT - or Zero Moment of Truth (Google, 2012). The fact is, that as people become accustomed to seeing you and your material, that they will eventually act upon it, because they are able to build the associations, the relevance. Google details that this will take up to 11 interactions before this latent activation.

How do you further create relevance for your own content, for the search engines themselves, to "help" them along, on terms of what the search engines present to you, when you make the search? The answer is "Content". You need to further elaborate your entire story online, what you do and everything you say. This can be accomplished through constant and consistent iterations of you, your brand, your messaging, and everything in-between. Your material, your stories, your videos, your photos, have to be more directed, as opposed to just randomly selected; you need to provide and build structure whereby you are create cohesive messaging across all formats and all channels.

Think of this as your "one big idea" for relevance; how do you always relate your business to the same, simple concept? You create a strategic architecture. This will be covered in this book. It will allow you to build your message consistently across all of your channels. Once you have clarity in terms of who you are, then you will be able to convey this appropriately and effectively to your audience.

Without relevance, businesses are meaningless. You do not exist. We strive towards creating the fabric that pulls everything together, online. This is editing. This is relevance. You will quickly become irrelevant if you don't understand this trend.

Why is this a trend? Primarily because it is the manner in which we convey information. We will continue to be bombarded by a magnitude of information on many levels. We will continue to be inundated by all types of information, and we will miss it. Or rather, your audience and customers will miss it and miss you if you don't "activate" them. It doesn't matter what you are putting out there, if nothing is seen, nothing is known. You will continue to be irrelevant, in an increasingly relevant world and landscape. You will fade into the background of irrelevancy.

Questions to ask your business:

1. What is the "one big idea" that allows my audience to edit down to what is important, quickly and easily?
2. Can you create consistent messaging throughout all my channels and website, to reduce the need to edit further and further? How?
3. How can I improve my delivery process to keep things consistent, clear, and a constant level of information?
4. What are some of the triggers that I have for my business that I can convey to the audience? Visuals? Text? Videos?
5. How many typical touch points do I have for all of my customers?
6. How do I make it easy for people to spot my message through all of the clutter that exists?
7. How do you personally "edit" your information in what you see and act on, online?
8. How do you think your audience will respond when viewing and encountering your content, your ideas?

The 3 Elements of Your Online Business – A Strategic Architecture for Digital Businesses

Successful online businesses have come to realise that there are a number of factors that help with the overall success or failure of a business online. While there is no magic formula, these factors, when combined together, build the actual relevance and importance of the business. Being able to put all of these factors together, simultaneously, is how you become the master of your digital domain. There are no short-cuts here.

You need to have an online relevance in order to have the search engines locate you. You need to be able to convert this relevance into awareness for your audience, to turn them into customers. You can build your relevance, and dominate your digital domain, with a clear understanding of all of the variables.

These can be broken down into 3 core ideas or insights; these are part of your entire digital domain, and part of a strategic architecture (that we will get you to develop in Step 1 – Strategy). This can be your fundamental understanding and strategy of what happens, and more importantly, what you need to do to make things happen. It is an understanding of the core of your business. This is where it starts:

1. Knowledge. The expertise, awareness and understanding of what you "talk" about in your industry.

2. Strategy. How you implement what you talk about. What steps do you take, how does your "system" work?

3. Awareness and Relevance. How, what you present, is relevant online and to your audience, and how aware customers or clients are of you and what you do.

Knowledge has the affect of either being too vague, or at the same time, being at such a level that it is simply not understood. Your knowledge, of you and your business, is what we are talking about; the knowledge of what you do, and what you plan to do. It is everything that you are trying to relay, whether it is the content of your new website, or the discussions on your webinars or newsletters. It is about what you know, and, more importantly,

How are you using some of the fundamental insights of a sound online strategy?

it is about how you convey that knowledge to your audience. It needs to resonate with your audience, to move them through your sales process.

Strategy is the fundamental direction that you are taking your business in. The problem is not so much you either have or don't have a strategy, or roadmap, but rather that the situation can simply be too complex for you and your business; this then is conveyed, unfortunately to your audience. If you have to explain exactly what your business does, and it takes people time to figure out what you do - then your strategy is too complex, and you will not be followed; people will lose interest. It's that simple. If you can reduce the complexity of your own strategy, so that people will quickly get that "a-ha" moment, then you are getting somewhere. Your business needs to be understood, not just by you, but also by your audience and customers. The opposite to this, however, is simply that it is too simple, and there is absolutely no direction to the business. People want to see that you and your business have aspirations, or that you have a mission, whether it is printed on your business cards or not. A business that does "nothing" or is not sure what they actually do is not a business that people will interact with. You will not be able to build and establish any trust. Without trust, there is no long-term business.

Awareness and Relevance is the third arm of your own Digital Domain. Awareness and relevance is that third tier - this is your audience. Today's online media world, presents a philosophical and existentialist tone, so if you are not relevant, you will not exist. Once you have built relevance, then you have awareness, and vice versa. Relevance is more about how the Search Engines actually place value on what you are producing, in a manner that then gets exposed to people searching for this. In other words, do you have what people are looking for? Relevance is quite "relative", so you need to explore all of the different avenues, and the search engines need to know how you actually rate. If the Search Engines don't "know" that you exist, then you simply do not.

There is a tremendous amount of complexity that could be introduced here, but it's not worth the effort. The most important factor about relevance and awareness, is that you are the one who controls this; you are the one who tells your story in all of your media channels, you are the one who creates the awareness of what you do, who you are, and everything else that is needed. Only YOU can control and distribute your relevance. It all starts with the essence of your business. The seed that you need to grow and nurture. You will be shown how to plant that seed, and how to create relevance and awareness in your digital domain.

These primary components actually form your overall strategy and understanding of how your business operates, and what exactly you need to accomplish online. Taking any of these items out, or even out of context, causes everything to collapse. This is your underlying strategic architecture. Combining all of these elements, in the right form and function, allows you to get to the "Online Empire Sweet Spot", where you can maximise your online business

What does this mean? Well, in summary, it means that you need to combine your knowledge and the knowledge of your business, with an underlying strategy. By doing this, you are able to create awareness and relevance for your business.

Now, the next obvious question is "how"? Well, this is actually the foundation of the entire framework that will be delivered to you shortly. Executing and implementing the framework will take some work, but by being diligent, you will get a very clear picture of what is needed within your framework, to build out your successful online empire.

Success is all about the framework and the process that will allow you to maximise your online business; get the most out of what you are trying to achieve. This framework is of course the Online Empire Project. This is how you will actually get your business to this proverbial "sweet spot". This is what this book is all about. By delivering a sound plan and executing it so that all components link or tie together, will see profitable success for your business.

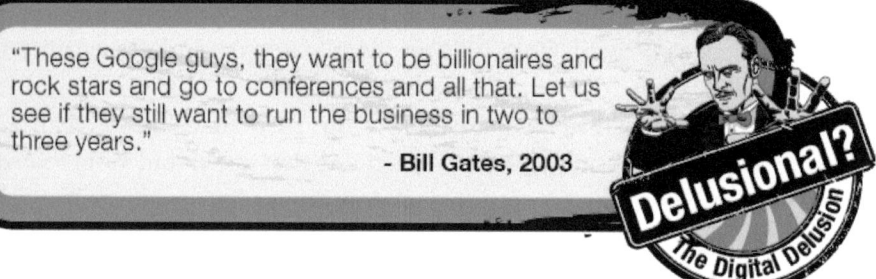

"These Google guys, they want to be billionaires and rock stars and go to conferences and all that. Let us see if they still want to run the business in two to three years."
- Bill Gates, 2003

The 17 Digital Components To Master Your Digital Domain

As you are aware, there are many different "components" of running your business online. You have probably encountered most, if not all, at some point in time. You might actually be working on some here and there, not really knowing why, or not really sure how you are going to get results from it.

There is a substantial amount of information that you need to know and learn in so many different areas, and many business leaders simply have not been able to organise themselves around these key concepts. Some of the delusions have been pointed out, so you really need to make an extra effort to understand what it is that you are trying to accomplish as a business. There is a lot of clutter online, as well as a significant amount of misinformation. Understanding what you need to know is critical to ensuring that you stay informed, and know what you need to do to make the right decisions. This of course is where a lot of the confusion of being online comes from.

Many businesses have "tested this", and "dabbled there", with little or no consistency throughout, or no solid foundation or framework to fall back upon. As a result of not being focused, they have not been able to achieve their business goals, or simply wondered around from place to place, supposedly seeing what will work and what doesn't. While this is a good way to develop some insight, you, as a business leader should be able to make online work, and make it work properly. If you don't have the framework or foundation, it simply will not work as well as it can.

The online world can be quite intimidating, and we don't really want to make any mistakes. Many are actually scared of trying. No one wants to be made to look like the fool. Then, when we do try, we usually make mistakes. As entrepreneurs in a new area, we don't want to mistakenly hit "the" button to shut off the internet.

Entrepreneurs are all for trying things out and seeing how they work for their businesses. What needs to happen though, is that you need to have a specific process that you go through in order to actually "test" things out.

Most importantly, you need to have a goal that you are trying to achieve for your "tests".

Within the Online Empire Framework, we will develop your plan for dealing with and actually implementing all of the various critical aspects of your new, revised online foundation. This structure will help you assign specific goals, as well as help create and understand the needed metrics of your business. The Online Empire Framework is a structure that takes all of these major components, reduce the complexity of it, and give you a process that will help you navigate all of these online elements. It doesn't matter whether or not you have tried something previously, as this new structure will allow you to be more open and flexible to getting things done online with your business. It helps you manage the confusion, and reduce the clutter.

Every online business requires a sound foundation. This book is about identifying what is important to you and your business, and what you can actively use. A comprehensive strategy can only be accomplished by combining all of the required elements. You may think that this is a lot of work, and you would be absolutely correct! This is not an easy task all around. The businesses that succeed, and succeed beyond their competition are the ones that have analysed each of these components, and put them in place accordingly.

The Online Empire Project methodology takes what is sometimes these seemingly disparate components, and puts meaning and value to each one, and how they interact and work together, to amplify what you are trying to achieve online. This is so that you can understand the significance of them, and further comprehend why you really need to put them in place. We are cutting through the clutter here, distilling it, so to speak, so that you can get done what you need to get done – run a successful business.

Each of these components is part of an effective online strategy. If you miss one of these, then you can miss out on your entire business. Online business is, and needs to be, like a finely tuned machine, with all of the different parts working in unison. There is no other way.

Digital Trends That Are Shaping Your Business

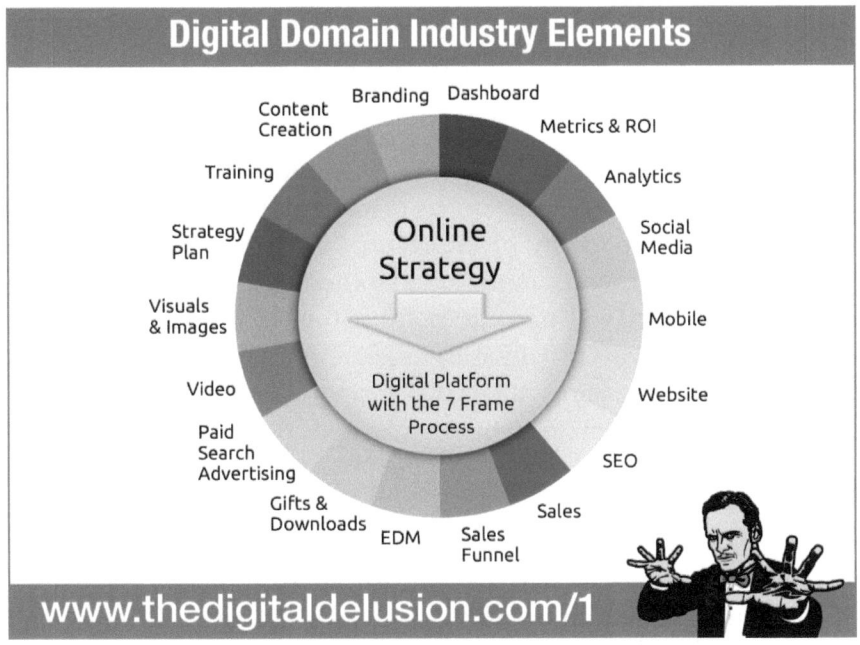

Which digital elements are you using effectively with your business online? How do they all interact with each other and your business?

The Online Empire Project that we will build for your business, combines a multitude of different components working together into the framework that will allow you to deliver on your business. Organising what you say and do is important to creating the clarity and direction that you need for your business. This is what the Online Empire Framework is about; it will help you get your businesses effectively organised for the online environment. It will help you manage your business so that you can then work on your business.

With this digital framework that we have created, you don't need to be an "expert" in any of these areas; you only need to understand how they relate and complement each other. They most certainly cannot be used in isolation, or the effect of each other one becomes irrelevant. Understanding how the components all fit together creates congruency as well, between all of the necessary elements of your business.

The core components that you will need, that will define your strategy, and how successful you become with your online empire, can be broken down further:

There needs to be a balance in all of the components. Many of the errors that businesses make is that they focus too intently on one or two of these components, at the jeopardy of the rest, in the hope that it will make a difference. They will spend countless dollars and time on SEO, for example, in the hope that they will make it to "The Top" or "Page 1" of Google; a goal that is fleeting, and usually misguided and ineffectual. The approach needs to be consistent, across all of the components, so that it is more of a complementary approach to all of the problems of online business.

If you have been in the online space for some time, you are more than likely quite familiar and aware with the various components presented, if even on an isolated, individual basis. More than likely you have given many of them a fair go. The framework that we are providing will assist further, as we have been able to combine all of these seemingly disparate concepts into a single methodology that includes everything of importance. It is further important to restate that these components need to work together, in unison, in order to be effective and get the results that you are looking for, for your business. This is what you will build upon in your Online Empire Project.

You don't need to be the expert; you need to know what you may be able to use, where and how, and what you may be missing in some areas. You need to know how to be able to leverage all of them together; this is where the Online Empire Project comes into play.

Now that you have a clearer idea of what exact components you need, take a self-assessment of where you are at. Out of all of the different components explained, which are the ones that you are working with directly? Which ones are ones that you need to work on further?

Digital Element	Do NOT Do 0 Pts	Unsure it is working 1 Pts	Think I've Got It 2 Pts	Awesome 3 Pts
Video				
Photos & image				
Search Engine Optimisation - SEO				
Social Networks & channels				
Pay Per Click or CPM advertising				
Analytics, KPI, Measurement and Insights				
Content Planning				
Blogging				
Auto responders/EDM/ email management				
Dashboard				
Webinars				
Ecommerce Engines, Sales Funnels & Online goals				
Affiliate marketing				
Core website				
Reporting & Management				
Local/mobile marketing				
Return on Investment - ROI				
CRM				
TOTAL				

www.TheDigitalDelusion.com

Questions To ask yourself:

1. From the list above, what elements of a complete, sound strategy are you missing? What ones do you have?
2. When will you implement the missing components?
3. What steps can you take towards putting these in place?
4. What has been your primary strategic focus for your business in the last 6 months? In the last year? What can you do differently in the next 6 months, and the next year?
5. If you had the opportunity to start from scratch, what would you include? What would you exclude?

Setting Online Goals

The framework that has been created in this book allows you, the business leader, to be able to organise your methods of online management. By putting things in a clear order and outlined manner, you will be able to understand what is important, and stay away from the things that are not. We're almost there.

The whole framework is only as strong as the sum of its parts. It is important that each of the components is looked at individually, yet worked on together, as a group. While some sites, for example, may not have an ecommerce capability, it is still as important, if not more so, to be able to create specific goals or outcomes of what your site needs.

Nothing can work properly unless you set up specific goals for your online environment. The components reviewed previously will help you shape what it is that you need to do. At the end of the day, however, you need to ensure that you have a very specific set of "goals" or targets that you put together, specific to your business. This will be very important to further building the structure around your business.

The importance of goals/actions is critical for ensuring that you have a means to improve and build upon what you are already building with your online business. Specific goals will help you begin to build a measurable level of interaction and engagement. Without goals, you really do not have a means for measuring whether you are actually successful or not. And, without a measure of success, you can question why you are in business.

Your goals can be such things as:

1. Download a free "gift", such as a free report, checklist, white paper, or anything that develops the contact with you and your audience.
2. Watch a specific video.
3. For clients to enter their email address to receive emails from your business
4. Make a purchase
5. Answer a survey
6. Go to a specific blog page

If you don't have any online goals or actions, then you really don't have a business. With no goals, there is nothing to achieve, and nothing to actually measure if you have made it or not. You need to set up some goals within your online domain to further enhance the online experience, as well as create measurable, quantifiable actions for your audience.

Questions to consider for your business

1. What current goals do I have on my website, if any? What are they?
2. How can I segregate specific goals or actions with my online plan and development?
3. What goals do I need to put in place? What is important to me and to my business?
4. What are some targets for each of these goals?
5. How will I implement my online goals?
6. How will I measure my online success?

> "There's just not that many videos that I want to watch."
> — YouTube cofounder Steve Chen, when the site featured only a few dozen videos, 2005

Delusional?

Learn how to identify the trends that affect your business online.

Scan QR Code or Link here: www.thedigitaldelusion.com/1

CHAPTER 6: The Online Empire Project — The Digital Delusion

"Professor Goddard does not know the relation between action and reaction and the need to have something better than a vacuum against which to react. He seems to lack the basic knowledge ladled out daily in high schools."

- The New York Times on Robert Goddard's pioneering rocket work, 1921

What You Need To Know

This chapter is defining the exact process and methodology that you will go through to fully overcome the deadly digital delusions.

You will learn:

1. The step-by-step guide on how to build your own digital platform for your business.

2. How to break down your own business in the online environment, so that you can rebuild it with a new framework.

3. What is important to your business, and how to leverage your own business.

Introduction to the Online Empire Project

You cannot afford to make mistakes online with your business. You need to be the immediate leader online, not a follower. You need to create a breakthrough online for your business or you won't be as profitable as you want to be, or worse case – you won't be around much longer. You need to transform your business, now.

Want to become remarkable online? Then start by thinking remarkably. The Online Empire Project will transform how you operate your business online - and how it makes business for you. This unique way of transforming your business online will create a remarkable breakthrough for you. If you could elevate your business to a new level of strategy and implementation online in a matter of a few steps, would you do it?

Think online. Think iconic changes and knowledge. Think innovation and implementation that will transform you and your business. Build your online influence now and grow your Online Empire.

What Is Empire Building Online About?

No matter where you go, or what your business is about, one thing is exceptionally clear these days. You and your business need to be online due to the technological society we are now entrenched in. Many businesses have tried it, and many have also failed.

Being online, while it is very ubiquitous, does not mean that every entrepreneur is ready and able. Or, simply ready and able to work online effectively. The brutal reality is that it is not a guarantee at success either.

Building your Online Empire is no different than building a business in the real world. There are so many different things to consider, and so many different ways to do them. The important thing is developing or using a system that allows you to organise and prioritise; something to help you structure what you do so that you have a measure to work with and manage the entire process.

If you are currently a business that operates strictly in the "bricks and mortar", then you need to make the move online, to truly create a distinct and unique level of operations with your customers and clients. If you are already online, then you need a specific, unique or individual way to fully engage and interact with your customers.

Being online is not as easy as just setting up a website and believing people will come. It doesn't work that way. The attention span of everyone is very short, and so in order to be successful online, it is important to create a new level of influence; a level of influence that allows you to be the leader in what you do and what you create online. Your overall implementation needs to be cohesive and clear across everything that you do.

The number one reason for businesses failing online is not that it is necessarily a bad idea, just that the strategy and implementation is far too broken up and piece-meal. It needs a sound, more effective strategy and implementation.

The overall goal for this book is about you becoming the business leader that you really are, the entrepreneur, and the success story; yet, one who is humble and realistic about the opportunities in front of them and their prospects – one that everyone can become, given some honest work and goal setting. This book is also an introduction into the concepts, systems and ideas of Online Empire Building.

A lot of business owners, entrepreneurs, and everyone in between, have all been to workshops on Social Media, Training in SEO, been consulted on with Paid Search, etc. etc. ad infinitum. The underlying problem, however, is that no one has ever created the needed integration of all of these online endeavours that you need to know, in order to build and sustain a growing online business. All of these factors cannot be measured and completed in isolation; everything needs to be reviewed and analysed and acted upon with the complete picture in mind.

One of the biggest problems that I have seen throughout the industry, has been the haphazard way in which most everything is hatched, without a complete understanding of the effects, or even how to amplify and connect it all. It is very disconnected. Many businesses would be looking for SEO improvements, yet not have a solid content plan in place. Likewise, advertising would be used, without a proper sales funnel to capture and respond to leads. The stories go on.

Anything less than an understanding of connecting and integrating everything, and your business will most certainly miss what is most important to getting that breakthrough that every business strives for. This is where the 'Empire Building Online' accounts for all of these seemingly disparate activities, and puts them in a clear and concise context that fits precisely with what your business needs for online success. You are taught everything you need to know to become successful online. It is of course up to you to implement.

You need to create a content, events-based, active model that gets people in your "door" and into your network. You need to have people contact you, based on what you do online, instead of the other way around. You need to increase your online influence and relevance.

You need to change the focus to one where you are setting up meetings online, discussing the business, getting people actually involved – all online. Telling your story with zest and panache. Developing an online presence that will attract more people directly.

You are not going to get significant fans or followers by doing the same thing over and over again, or posting the same material. It is not just about making postings onto social media sites, and finding interesting articles to share, and "cute" stories to tell; you need to do more.

Building Your Online Empire

All of the things that you need to do online to build your online empire, can all be completed within this 7 step program.

The 7 Frames or Steps covers absolutely everything that you and your business need, to make that significant, remarkable breakthrough online. It does not matter what business you are in, or whether or not you have already been online, or even if you are just starting out.

The purpose of the 7 Frames is to create your actual strategy and foundation – put all of the building blocks that you need for a successful business, in place and ready. You will need to continue to build and implement on this over time. Social media and online business is not simply about "firing and forgetting"; it needs to be addressed on a consistent, regular basis so that you are continually able to make advances in your business and stay ahead of your competition.

This framework has a unique structured and strategic approach that covers all of the components that work in the online world. Consider it a new marketing course for online implementation. It is not only a set list of clear and executable instructions, but also a clear and underlying strategy that when implemented correctly and diligently, will lead to your business success.

How to Become Awesome Online: The Basics of Building Your Online Business Breakthrough.

These are the components and framework that we will be using for building your online empire. Combined, these steps cover material that is critical to how you organise, manage and operate your business online. It is about building and enhancing your influence online, with all of the tools and resources that you have at your disposal.

Frame 1	Online Empire Building "Disco" Discovery, trend Analysis and Strategic Alignment
Frame 2	Content Planning, Creation and Development. Words still "Rock"
Frame 3	Social Networking and Sharing. There's more than just 'The' Facebook.

Frame 4	Video & Visuals. Hollywood and the Paparazzi goes online.
Frame 5	Website Alignment & Congruency. Create and evolve your web presence.
Frame 6	Online Lead Strategies. How to create the sales funnel that works.
Frame 7	Advanced Online Empire business building strategies and tactics. Advertising, Analytics and Dashboards.

Throughout this book, your knowledge and awareness of what works best for you and your business online through this process, will be expanded on.

Building Your Online Empire

How would you feel if people were easily able to find and approach you online, to ask questions; and that you were quickly able to nurture them into solid leads that then convert in sales or additional team members for your network?

The goal of your business is to get people interested in what you do; which will then generate revenue and your bottom line ROI. It doesn't matter whether or not you are a direct selling business, an online retail ecommerce business, or even just a fan site – everything that you need to do online needs to make business sense, otherwise it is just a hobby.

More importantly, you want people to be able to find you, and to quickly recognise "you" for who you are. This is your own personal brand – success, freedom, entrepreneurism at its finest.

The problem is that everyone is doing the same thing. There is nothing different out there; just a lot of noise.

This is about to change for you and your business. It's not just about Facebook either. It's not about Twitter. It's not about Linkedin.

You are probably already trying to use social media in a number of different ways for your business. And, you're probably finding that it doesn't really work – at least not in the way that you had hoped, or were told. Is this strategy really working for you, the way that you want it to? What is your Return On Investment?

As you have already come to realise, social media is in fact only a means to an end. What really needs to happen is that you need to build and demonstrate your "expertise" amongst everyone else in your industry. You need to develop your brand and experience around this. You need to build your key influence online. And it is not all about social media.

You Are Your Own Brand

You and your business are a personality worth "exposing" to the world. You need to influence and inspire your community with your brand. Your brand is about being in control of your lifestyle, being successful, being passionate. This is your influence that can be built with your business. This is your online empire waiting at the gates.

This book shows you the process that you need to know to properly build your business and engage your audience online – how to build your online influence by defining:

1. How to define the best channel and social network for your business.
2. How to develop your own specific content through videos and webinars, and utilising other tools that actually work.
3. How to develop the knowledge base of your audience and lead base, so that you become the expert in your direct selling area.
4. How to learn to enhance your lead collection and generation system. So you've got customers or clients coming to your website? Learn what it takes to actually take them to the next step.
5. How to combine existing strategies with what you already know and do.

6. How to work with the major trends of SEO and social media, and every other type of online marketing that is out there.

7. How to create an effective online empire building strategy that grows with your business.

8. How to organise and utilise a detailed and aggressive strategy and management plan in order to become the leader in your field.

9. How to build and maximise your online influence, and convert that to users and partners for you and your business network, to build your business online.

10. How to focus on what will work for you and show you how to communicate and leverage that information extensively, in all facets of your business.

11. How to develop your online "influence", relevance, and, most importantly, get you customers or clients.

12. How to develop a comprehensive content plan that allows you to find your complete "voice", and deliver it in a timely and informative manner to your complete audience.

Frame By Frame - Building an Online Breakthrough For Your Business

The Online Empire methodology requires a new look at how you accomplish things online, and how you integrate these activities into your current business. This methodology is not about starting from scratch, but rather putting the pieces that you already have into a manageable and executable program that works for you and your business. The answers and details come from how your current business operates and implements online activities. You are simply provided the structure and framework to make your business function online.

Frame	Focal Point	Theme	Core Criteria and General Activities To Complete
1	Discovery	Online Empire Building "Disco" Discovery and Strategic Alignment	• Audit and Understanding of Current Capabilities • Establishing a strategic architecture • Social media strategy review and questionnaire • Social Media workshop review • Customer identification and discovery
2	Content Strategy	Content Planning, Creation and Development. Words still "Rock"	• Building Your Story online • Designing your content • Scheduling, Timing & Delivery • Concurrent Needs of SEO • Press Releases and Media development
3	Social & Sharing	Social Networking and Sharing. There's more than just 'The' Facebook.	• Channel Prioritization and Selection • Channel set-up and establishing your foundation • Channel strategies to get maximum value for your business • Cross channel propagation • Coordinating and scheduling your content.

4	Video & Visual Content	Video & Visuals. Hollywood & the Paparazzi goes online	• The importance and ease of video • How to create video content • Creation & Production • Key Performance factors • Webinars to successful businesses • Placement of video channels and cross promotion • Setting up your SEO Requirements • Usage and placement of images • Technical requirements of images • Importance of image types • Creation and sizes • Management of images and sharing
5	Website Alignment	Website Alignment & Congruency. Create and evolve your web presence	• Understand and implement website goals • Restructure site as needed for "gifts" and "product for prospects" • Create congruency • Embodiment of proper sales funnel • Back-end SEO • Content Development • Mobile Responsive • Local Mapping enabled

6	Online Lead & Traffic Strategies	Online Lead Strategies. How to create the sales funnel that works.	• Lead Development – Ascending Transaction Model • Webinars as lead generators • Product development in the online environment • Social Networking advanced lead generating strategies • EDM activities and list building • Content distribution in your lead generation • Effective Online Sales funnels • Affiliate Marketing
7	Advanced Online Strategies	Advanced Online Empire business building strategies and tactics. Advertising, Analytics and Dashboards	• Online media buying and advertising on Google adwords, Linkedin & Facebook • Content channels to expand your reach and your control • Online Response strategies • Analytics & Measurement • Measurement, Tools & Dashboards to use to control your online influence and response

Do you understand the 7 Frames that can make your business more effective online, to provide you with a complete and comprehensive digital platform?

What You Need to Do to Engage in Building Your Empire Online

Building your online empire is not easy, it will take some significant effort in order to be able to put it in place. This process is unique in that a framework has been created to allow you to put all of the various aspects linked to your business, in place. Breaking everything down into the fundamental building blocks will create the structure that you need to properly organise your online efforts, and build your success. This will build your foundations, your infrastructure.

With the mountains of information out there, as well as the delusion of guru's and experts, it is necessary to cut through all of the misinformation and get down to the basics. This is what this framework provides; simple, effective steps that you can detail and complete on your own, and with your own resources. You don't need a guru either; everything that you need is right here, and ready to go.

How Does This Fit With Your Business?

The Online Empire Project framework is an enabling tool to help you leverage what you already do online, and puts everything into a simple methodology that works specifically for your business.

The important thing to know is that you do not need to start a new business; you do not need to start from scratch. This methodology allows you to improve your existing business, to help you develop a new, strategic approach to all of your online activities.

Frame #1: Strategy Development
Learn how to craft a key strategy to guide all of your online activities

What is it?

"Frame 1" consists of discovering what your business is about. It is important to delve into the brand essence of who you are as a business, and what you do. How do you understand and discover your brand essence? You need to ask and answer the question "what are you about"? Then, translating what you think and do into a strategic architecture that will help you align all of your digital and online activities.

Do you understand the micro trends that are growing and shaping your actual business? What about your customer? Are they "following" the same trends that you are? While it may seem like a simple problem, as a business leader you need to ensure that the trends around you and your business are complementary to what your customer and audience is looking for, otherwise your business will eventually fade out.

The strategy is the over-riding plan that allows you to align what you do online, with your actual business. Strategy is not the same as actual "tactics"; a strategy is the overall plan that you are undertaking, not the specific activities that you will carry out.

You need to be able to have congruency between what you think you are about, what you want to be about, and what your customer thinks you are about. Only once you have this alignment, will you be able to build your breakthrough success.

How does it work?

Through a series of strategic thought exercises, you will come to quickly understand that what you are about is sometimes different from what you perceive yourself to be, or what your customer perceives you to be as well. From this thought exercise; you will be able to see the forest through the trees – and really understand the essence of your business.

The understanding needs to be more about what the under-riding philosophies of your business. Sometimes, digging deep into what you're not about, will allow you to create the extra depth to a better understanding of your company. Taking a further, deeper look into what your customer sees is also instrumental in determining more of your essence.

As previously covered, a "trend" is a long-lasting basis of activity that an audience will partake in, such as certain types of new music, specific "new" activities, such as kite-boarding. Trend analysis is capturing the essence of your audience in what they do, say, behave, purchase, etc. This is significantly different from the essence of your business, and needs to be understood as such.

It is also important to recognise the difference between a trend and a "fad". A fad is a short-term audience trigger or activity, such as a "one hit wonder" song, or a toy, such as a Ferbie.

Knowing what trends exist within your audience is critical to ensure that the products and services that you are offering have the potential to last for as long as possible, and hence allow your business to remain IN business.

What You Need To Do

You will need to review and answer the following questions:

1. What are 'we' (your business) about?
2. What do 'we' do best?
3. What makes it work?
4. What is the value that we will provide to our customers? Today, tomorrow, next year?

5. What are we good at? What are the skills/competencies of your business?

6. What are we good at? What do we need to be better at?

7. What is your "experience" about? What will your visitors take away from your website?

8. What does your customer "look" like? What are the customer baselines and trends, such as Who is your customer? What are they doing? Where are they doing it? What are they looking for? How will you engage them in their space?

What you need to do next:

1. Take the answers to your fundamental questions, and create three key pillars or concepts and understandings about your business. This then becomes your "Strategic Architecture".

2. Use your strategy and understandings across all of your implementation, to create congruency and a sense of "self".

What Is It?

Content is in essence, what you post and put on the web. Everything that you have ever produced, gets indexed, and then relates to what you and your company has put online. It's not just about your blog, either. It's about everything that is about you and your business online. If you haven't posted anything, then guess what? There really is nothing around to tell your story online. You are not building your knowledge without content. You will be 'invisible' without content. Content is not the "king" either; think of it as your muse.

While content also contains photos, images and videos, which will be covered in Frame 3 and Frame 5, the core content at this stage is the actual text and words that you put in place, linked to what your business is about. This applies not only to your website, but in everything that you produce online, including the text on your website.

Content is the core of Search Engine Optimisation (SEO). SEO does not need to be excruciatingly difficult or complex. SEO is really just about telling your story online, yet connecting it to everything else. The important thing to remember is that without content, the search engines will not find you, and hence, your customers will not be able to find you either. You will be irrelevant.

Online writing is surprisingly under utilised by the majority of businesses and entrepreneurs. It should, in essence, be considered as fundamental as existing activities, like sales, operations and marketing. It is imperative that writing about your business be prioritised to the same level as these activities, as it carries the same (and more, for that matter) overall weight in your business.

Having a personal or company blog is critical for the further success of your business, as it creates the linking point for all of your content that you subsequently create online and share with others. If you do not have a company blog, then you need to create one. If you do not know how to write one, then you need to learn.

"Blogging" is unfortunately viewed by most as 'something else' that does not help with the building of the business. This attitude needs to change in order to maintain relevance. You need to write as if your business depends on it, as guess what? It actually does.

The main thing preventing you from writing and producing content is probably not that you can't write, but rather you are not sure of what you should write or talk about. Correct? This is called the "white-board" syndrome - getting ideas out of your head is sometimes the hardest part. However, once you start, things begin to move forward quickly. The way to

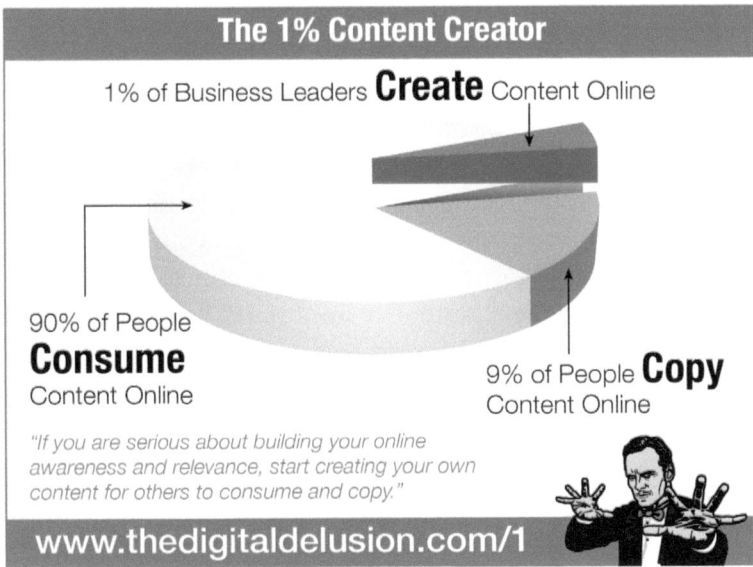

How much content are you generating for your business?

make producing content easier and much more effective and timely, is by looking more at what you do, and putting some structure to it.

Your blog is connected to everything, and if not, then you need to make this adjustment. Your core content also consists of your website, social media, video, visuals, gifts and downloads; these will be covered later. Your blog is a distribution channel that needs to be at the core of what you do, from where everything else flows, including:

1. Video discussions
2. Press releases & media
3. Images and sharing
4. Social and sharing connection
5. Syndication (other bloggers/posts)
6. Email content marketing
7. Industry news and publications
8. Document hosting

How Does It Work?

The search engines are constantly scouring the Internet for content about you and everything related to your business, and, more importantly, your competition. This is your "relevance". This is all about how your customers are actually able to find you online. If you don't post your own content, then someone else will, and your business will not be able to develop online, as there will be no relevance. Content is important, but it also needs to be relevant to you and your business, as well as attributed to you and your business. This is how you stop being 'invisible'.

A general industry 'understanding', is that about 90% of online content is just consumed amongst everyone, and created by a select few. Nine percent is actually copied and re-published by others, for such things as social media links, etc. This leaves a surprising 1% of content that is actually created as the source by writers, entrepreneurs, etc. Once you realise this, it is easy to understand why creating your own content can really develop your business and relevance online, as not many people are actually doing it – most people are simply copying.

Content will raise the awareness of you and your organisation; it's as simple as that. You will be able to kick-start a conversation internally or to wider public audiences, as well as capitalise on a topic trend to introduce your company as a ranking expert. You can also supply news about your industry or company that is no longer provided by mainstream media. And, you can get information to vitally interested niche groups about your product or service. Content helps others find you and your business, whatever that may be.

What You Need To Do

Understanding content is the easy part. Building content is the part that will take some work and dedication. The other core aspect of content is actual "curation"; how you build, maintain, reuse and repurpose your content. You will need to become proficient in the following:

- Content Strategic Alignment. How does the content fit with your own specific goals and strategic plans?
- Developing Themes for your business.
- Content Development
- Content Scheduling
- Attribution & Setting Up Authorship
- Setting up a Blog
- Press Releases
- Content Curation and Usage (frequency)
- How to write shareable content
- How to place content across the Web
- How to write content that is more about building a community and does more than just sell

- Develop and understand your customer. Create personas or personalities that are your ideal customer.

What about keywords? Yes, keywords are important, but keyword "stuffing" is not going to work. What is the "key" about keywords? Talk about what you are best at, and your own keywords will appear. What is the content of your normal, day-to-day conversations? These are the same conversations that you will have online, complete with all of your own keywords. If you don't think that you know what keywords you need to use, then here are some tools for researching further:

- SocialMention.com
- www.stumbleupon.com/tag
- Technorati.com/tag
- Ads.youtube.com/keyword_tool
- www.hashtags.org

Keep in mind that the content on your entire digital domain needs to be conversational. People will be reading about what you have, and making an assessment of you based on this.

Here are some types of content that you can create:
- Articles
- Blogs
- Case Studies
- Digital Newsletters
- ebooks
- Email
- Images
- Info-graphics
- Microsites
- Mobile content

- News releases
- PDFs
- Podcasts
- Research
- Slide shows
- Social
- Traditional media
- Video
- Webinars
- White papers/special reports

What to do next

You will need to review and answer the following questions/exercises:

1. Using your refined strategy, list 6 core topics of information that you will discuss online.

2. Further separate your 6 core activities into three sub-topics or topic specialties.

3. Create a content calendar. For each subtopic, complete content activities and writing each week. Post each of these as blog posts within your company or personal blog. Include all other types of content in your overall content plan.

4. Identify the various personas that are part of your audience and customer base. Who are they? What do they do? How can you describe them?

5. Share your blog posts across all the channels that you will develop.

6. After 18 weeks, create new topics, subtopics and a new calendar.

7. Develop a list of 12 topical keywords that you will use; these will form part of your core content. They are what you will need to use throughout all manifestations of your content.

Frame #3: Social & Sharing
Understanding what you need for a proper social media engagement

What Is It?

Social networking is about connecting you and your business with your customers and potential customers through your social media channels. Connecting with your audience, however they are defined, is critical to your overall business success. Without an audience, there is no business, no matter how good you might be, or how perfect your product or service actually is.

Social networking is, however, just a tool. It is one tool of many that you need to build an effective online business. It is a medium that you can use to interact and engage with your audience. It is, in essence, no different than the use of television to broadcast content, ideas, and of course advertising.

The significant difference today, is that social networking is more about a two-way form of interaction with an audience and brands online. No longer is marketing "pushed" onto the viewer. Now, people are only interested in what they find and "pull" towards themselves, based on their interests and activities. This is all part of the relevance aspect.

Brands that are able to leverage this over-riding philosophy of social media being a tool, and have allowed content and ideas to be "pulled" by their audience, are the ones that are able to build very large communities online in the social networking space. They are able to interact and engage with their audience in a manner that promotes the concepts of sharing information and knowledge across their full product range and activities. 'Good' brands using social media don't "sell"; their audience "buys", based on how they feel about the brand.

There are a significant number of channels in social media that allow for this participative, opt-in marketing. As part of the strategy of your business, it is important to understand where your audience will primarily be. Where do they work? Where do they play? While Facebook is one of the tools that you might consider, it is important to understand that there are other tools that may work better for your business. The further evolution of social networking means that the available channels are becoming more and more specialised as time progresses. Find out where your audience is, and the then you can build out your specific channels.

How Does It Work?

Social media is the essence of sharing in our online, connected world. It is critical to be able to understand what connections you need to know to grow your business, and how to implement these.

Enabling a specific strategy of business building online requires that the sharing side of the online interactions are developed and leveraged.

In order to create an engaging and inviting environment, it is necessary to create content that is related to what your audience enjoys and understands. Your message has to resonate with your audience or it will simply not be able to sustain itself.

While social media channels seem to change quite regularly, there are some primary categories of channels that can be used, including blogs, micro blogging, social networks, image sharing, and video sharing.

These are some of the basic steps for developing and building your social media channels:

1. Understanding the basics and types of social networking, and how each one may work in your business.
2. Channel analysis – knowing what to use, when, etc. Where is your customer?
3. What specific 'social' needs to your require for your business? How does this fit with your overall, revised strategy?
4. Setting up your channels so that they are connected.
5. Content Development - placing your content everywhere.

6. Community Development. Look at sharing not only your content, but also the content of others. Share in the conversation with others in your "neighbourhood".

What You Need To Do Next.

1. Decide on what social network channels will work best for you, your business and your audience.
2. Connect your social media channels with your website and your online goals.
3. Allow for sharing in a bi-directional manner. Cross-promote content. Connect all your social media channels with each other, and with your primary website and sales funnel.
4. Use your detailed content plan – include topics and specific dates.
5. Post to your core knowledge platform. Become the expert in your area.
6. Distribute your content across your social channels.
7. Complete all of the "about me" and SEO sections in all of your social channels so that you can create the necessary links and relevance for you and your business.
8. Implement your content plan. Post to your schedules and post content on all of your social channels.
9. Interact and connect with other, complementary businesses; comment and complement on what they are saying.

Video and visuals are critical to conveying your specific company branding. It represents you personally, as well as your brand. Ask yourself this question: how effective is your branding online? It comes down to how you convey what is visual about you and your brand. Does it convey your messages clearly and concisely?

And no, branding is not just about your logo. It is your visual identity. More importantly, branding needs to be broken down into the simple visuals, as well as video content.

Part 1: Video

What Is It?

Video is one of those technologies that is far under utilised across the web. Did you know that YouTube gets 3 Billion views per day?

Video however, actually creates a greater understanding of a person, their business, and their personality. It is a way of connecting that simply cannot be matched in any other medium. It is a relatively easy way for people to get in "touch" with you and your expertise.

Every business and entrepreneur has content that can be translated into a video format. This allows for sharing content across all channels that you then have, with just a link. Video allows you to step above your competition, to become a showcase of you and your skills, and your business.

YouTube is not the only channel out there. There are many other video sharing sites, many that most people have not encountered yet. Have you heard of Vimeo, for example? It is a very practical tool that can be used for hosting and sharing your videos.

How Does It Work?

Video is visual. It is where you create the content that you can lead people through, and instruct and share your knowledge, to increase your relevance. Whether it is about training or simple display of knowledge and expertise, it can be relayed very effectively through video.

As mentioned, video is far under utilised, so this means you can still take advantage of what you are creating online, in terms of video. Social media is about creating a connection with yo ur audience. As such, video allows you to showcase who you are, and what you are about. Whether you are discussing how to create amazing photographs, or how to run a training session for your business, video is what you need to enable to reach your audience, and to beat your competition.

Video for video's sake is not that effective. It is necessary to plan ahead and produce relevant content that represents who you are and what you do. You can then leverage your videos in weekly episodes, which people will come to rely on you from you. Create and use video as part of your overall content planning.

What You Need To Do.

Here are some key concepts that are important for creating effective videos and video content:

You and Your "Brand" - Know yourself; present yourself as you are, along with all of your quirks and idiosyncrasies; your individual character. Don't worry about what people will think. Just film it! Present yourself as your brand and what you have to offer.

Timings - YouTube analytics consistently show that people are more likely to click play on a shorter video, and more likely to 'stick' with a video if the end is in sight. For example, if you publish a six-minute video, people will stop watching at the four-minute mark, but they'll likely stay to the end of a five-minute video. Always be as concise as possible and within a specific timeframe that gets your points across. Aim for roughly 2-3 minutes per video.

Great audio, Video & lighting - Be sure not to neglect clear audio over video, or adequate lighting. All aspects need to be the best that you can afford. Quality is paramount. While non-professional videos are sometimes cute and quaint, better quality does mean that they will become more valuable over time. Don't be afraid to start though, even if you don't have high-end equipment and lighting. Worst case, ensure that you have good quality audio. Poor audio is the best way to have someone desert your video very quickly.

Accountability - Set goals and timelines and stick to them. If not, involve someone you can trust to help keep you on track. Create a video at least once every week or every two weeks. Schedule the same time and same place, so that your audience starts to get in tune with your consistency.

Knowledge - This is part of the initial 3 strategy components. Keep your knowledge base working so that it is productive and beneficial to your audience. Avoid jargon and technical information that says too much.

What you need to do next:

1. Plan your video outreach – develop your content plan as detailed in Frame 2, but specifically for video.

2. Creating a weekly schedule that fits into an "episode" of your special content.

3. Establish your channels on YouTube, Vimeo, or other hosting services.

4. Film your episodes on a weekly basis; record short videos of about 2-3 minutes. Set one day a week to upload your weekly episode, and ensure this is done.

5. Broadcast your video and share it across all of your other channels. Use your blog as a primary means of sharing your videos, and then

link into all of your other channels. Promote the video in all of your status updates, and all of your posts.

6. Always complete the full descriptions, tags and keywords for your videos, whether you are hosting them yourself, or on YouTube or Vimeo. Even consider getting the video transcribed, which is now offered on YouTube. The search engines can't actually 'see' video, hence you need to be as descriptive as possible, to enhance your relevance.

Part 2: Visuals

What Is It?

Images are the "currency" of the online world. Images are everywhere. Today's society is a very visual culture; we will take a picture or view an image over words any day. With online businesses they need to use and leverage images in all their activities.

Even if you think that your business is not necessarily "picture friendly", it is critical that you move towards increasing the level of image representation, both from a website basis, and also from the social networking side of things.

While it does change from time-to-time, recent statistics from Facebook indicate that the items that have the highest share equity are in fact images. Then follows links, and finally, text status updates.

Moving into a visual world online for your business can be done quite promptly, as there are many services and apps that will help and assist with developing your message.

Here are some critical aspects that need to be developed for use of photographs in your online business:

- The importance of images for sharing - Photos can quickly move from user to user.

- SEO & images - Search engines are not yet able to actually "see" photos, so you need to enhance them with text based referencing for search engines.

- Tools & apps for images - What app works for your business and your user base/audience?

- Taking good photos - If you need help with photography, take a quick photo course. Utilise free photo editing software.

- Use of Word Art - Convert your infamous quotes of the day, into word art as an actual picture.

- Creative uses - Look at how photos can be used in all aspects of your business. How do you convey your marketing message photographically?

- Branding - All images that that you own and create need to have your own branding. This allows for future views to be able to re-connect with you and your brand.

- Infographics - These create the opportunity for unique, branded, knowledge-based graphics. Look at how you can implement these types of images to further enhance your business.

How Does It Work?

There are many different photo sharing social networks, apps and programs that allow you to increase your level of brand awareness. One of the most popular photo sharing applications for the mobile generation is Instagram, where images can be converted with a filter to further enhance them for sharing to others.

Facts about instagram and photos that attract more attention:

http://www.forbes.com/sites/roberthof/2013/09/08/so-much-for-facebook-ruining-instagram-it-just-hit-150-million-monthly-active-users/

http://www.dailymail.co.uk/sciencetech/article-2492885/Want-likes-Instagram-Make-sure-photos-BLUE-Images-containing-colour-receive-24-attention.html

Additionally, as photos are shared online, it is important to ensure that your photos generate positive SEO, through a variety of methods. These include:

1. Save the filename as your brand name or website name, along with 2 or 3 adjectives that describe what the photo is actually about.
2. Always put a watermark on your photographs with your web address.
3. Utilise tags, alt text, meta descriptions and other text based descriptions and referencing to further allow search engines to locate your images. Include your URL in all of your positioning.

What You Need To Do.

Answer the following questions about your business:

1. What photo-sharing, social media site works for your business?
2. How can you use photographs of your business? What products do you have? How does your service business photograph activities?
3. How will you name the photos and use tags to further generate SEO relevance?
4. How will you put an emphasis on photos in your regular social network channels?

What you need to do next.

1. Create an image database that is online and connects with your URL. It also needs to detail out all of the photos and images that you use for sharing.
2. Add visuals to your content plan and implement them across all of your channels.
3. Create incentives for sharing your visual content. What ideas are you conveying in your visuals? How do they work and how do they interact?

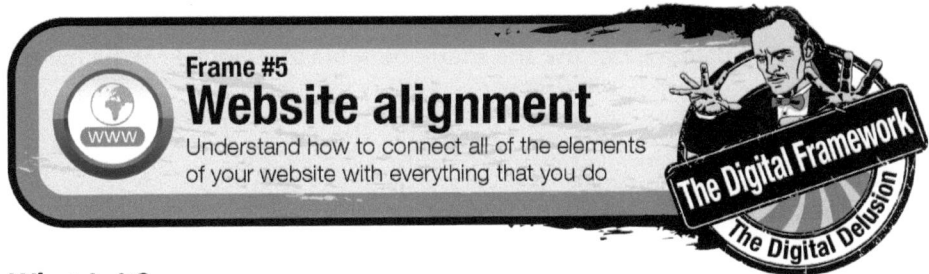

What Is It?

Your website is the heart of your business. It is not the 'soul', however. While you may have all of your social media channels in place, all your video uploads performing, all your photos loading on instagram, everything relates back to what your website does, and how well it performs. Your website is where you will actually make money for your business; it is like the lifeblood of your online business. Without it, you are simply, non-existent. It does need all of the supporting infrastructure, in order to make it work. It won't work on its own.

While you can have a Facebook page, it is difficult to run a business completely on Facebook. Your own webpage gives you the ability to create your own environment, under your own terms; it conveys the essence of you and your business.

What would happen if Facebook suddenly closed it's doors, or states to wane? Even more so - are you able to control your own environment if you work entirely on Facebook? While the risk is small, it is important to understand what is needed here. You need to be able to control your own environment. There are many issues with privacy, design, and simple control that you will be giving up if you just deal with a single platform such as Facebook.

Your website is your own online digital identity; your website is your foundation and your home base. It's where the majority of purchases are made and where people search you out. Think of it as being no different than your own retail store, business, or coffee shop. While you may rent space from the landowner, you are free to conduct your business how you want, without specific constraints. You may situate your business in a shopping centre to gain the extra traffic, but again, you still run your own business. Facebook and your website are the same thing – you need to truly own your own business, but use the many benefits that Social Media has to offer.

How Does It Work?

Your website needs to align with all of your various channels. It is your primary channel and platform that everything is built upon. It needs to be first class, and it needs to be put together with order and a clear understanding of your overall online business strategy.

If you already have an existing site, you need to ensure that you create the alignment needed across every other channel and every page. This means that your web pages need to be congruent, and that the information is consistent across all channels and platforms. The message that you deliver needs to be clear, but importantly, it needs to be aligned with everything that is about you and your business. You also need to start to think about your sales funnel, and how you will put these pieces in place as well.

If you are starting from scratch, you will need to take into account everything that is being developed in the Online Empire Project.

Keep your website "clean" from a design perspective. Your website needs to reflect the overall branding that you have and are developing over time. Ensure that you have exit and entry points, and that you are developing strong primary and secondary calls to action to enter your sales funnel.

What You Need To Do.

Your online presence must be congruent across everything that you build online. This includes, more particularly, what is happening on your website.

Take a look, and ensure that this is what you have:

1. All social channels need to be displayed. They need to be connected, but also to ensure that people can share your content with their own community.
2. Ensure that you have sharing capabilities across all of the different components of your website. Share to Twitter, Pinterest, Facebook, or whatever channels you are using.
3. Include your blog in your own pages. Use this as your PR message, as well as for your content distribution.
4. Your visuals should match between all different channels.
5. Ensure that your analytics package is setup, and you have specific goals embedded into the process.
6. Create your sales funnel, with specific downloads, webinars, and of course, purchase points throughout all of the different stages of your site.
7. Create easy to use navigation.
8. Use lots of visuals, as well as key videos for your pages.
9. Understand your overall strategy and how it affects your website.
10. Regularly change your "static" content on your pages, usually at least every 1-2 months (this is besides the weekly updates of your blog).
11. Avoid the use of Flash, as this is not as easily referenced by the Search Engines.
12. Complete the back-end SEO, such as using complete Meta descriptions.
13. Always utilise your core keywords throughout your website.
14. Feature video that highlights your sales, purpose, goals, core business, etc.

Additionally, there will be other aspects and activities that you will need to take into consideration, when aligning, implementing and utilising your website.

Linking - Establishing and creating links to your website, complementary sites and all of your social networking channels. This is "connecting" all of your various channels and activities across everything online.

Local Marketing - As mapping and GPS becomes an integral part of people's day to day lives, your business can leverage this capability effectively in all of your online activities, including developing and enhancing your SEO.

Mobile Marketing - 91% of the world population has a mobile device, and 51% uses smart phones to gather information from around the Internet. It is expected that by the end of 2013, there will be more mobile devices than people (www.supermonitoring.com, 2013). More and more people are mobile enabled, to allow them to be constantly connected at all times. How do you connect with your audience in the mobile environment, as part of your brand experience?

Building a website is not an easy task. It needs to be viewed and designed from multiple angles and multiple uses. Here are some of the basic elements that you need to accomplish in the actual design stage of your website:

1. Headline – What is the main focus of your website?
2. Sub headline – What are the other details or messages that you need to convey?
3. Benefits – Why would people do business with you?
4. Primary Calls-to-Action – This is where your goals come into play. What specific actions do you want your visitors to undertake? Utilise 2-3 calls to action that reflect the various buying stages of your audience.
5. Features – What are the features of your products that you want your audience to quickly recognise?
6. Customer Proof – If you have any customer testimonials, use them to build your credibility.
7. Success Indicators – What makes your solution the best out there?

8. Navigation – Ensure that any person can get to any point in your site within 2 clicks.

9. Supporting Images - All your visuals need to support your overall messaging.

10. Gift Offer – Provide some initial information at no cost or obligation to your intended audience, to help begin entry into your sales funnel.

11. Resources – This is your own library. How do they download your checklists, source lists, guides, etc?

12. Secondary Calls-To-Action – Connect and engage with your social media channels. Ensure clients can contact you quickly and easily, and that they can sign up to your email list, or download some key knowledge pieces.

13. Conduct an SEO scorecard. Look at: keyword targeting, title tags, meta descriptions, internal anchor test, inbound links, outbound links, image alt text, social links, social sharing widgets. Look at using the newer form of SEO, including schema.org

14. Create a "Responsive" site that allows can automatically configure itself for mobile devices and tablets.

15. Create landing pages that allow you to create niche content.

A properly designed and developed website will usually take 4 weeks to create. This is usually as a result of getting all of the content and designs created, as well as the back-end configuration for ecommerce.

Your website needs to be part of a constantly evolving process. It will never be "finished", in that it should be a constantly developed by adding new content, and adjusting the different aspects of your site. Why? Well, the search engines also look at how often your site gets updated, as this is usually a good indicator of currency. Refine it more and more as you go along, knowing that you do not need to start with the perfect website.

What you need to do:

Ask yourself the following questions about the overall design, development and implementation on your website:

1. Will you be completing the work internally or externally?
2. Will you be using a professional web designer?
3. What key features do you want and need for your website?
4. How will you generate leads and sales from your site?
5. What type of content will you distribute? What free gifts or promotions will you offer to visitors?
6. How will you track all your visitors?
7. What are your site goals?

What you need to do next:

1. Align your website with your new strategy, content plan and website goals.
2. Write a website specification that allows you to fully explain the types of features and capabilities you want your site to have.
3. Start building, adding to or re-designing your website. Continue to develop and grow it over time. Keep it live, interesting, visual and dynamic.

What Is It?

Despite the Internet being and becoming a premium sales kit for every business and entrepreneur, there are a lot, if not all, businesses who are not actually harnessing what it is that they do online in terms of a cohesive sales process. Understanding that your business needs to treat each and every fan, customer/client or person, as actually part of the sales process, or sales funnel, is critical for online success.

A sales funnel is the process where you bring your web users closer towards an action or a sale. Not everything can necessarily be sold online, however, it is still quite critical to be able to bring every person as close as you can to the end point or result. A sales funnel can be directing the user towards a specific action, such as downloading an ebook, opening a specific sales page, making an email request for a test drive, or anything in between.

If you operate an online ecommerce store, then your obvious outcome is the final paying transaction. However, it is important to understand that your customer is not always ready to make a purchase through your online channel. In that case, it is important to feed them into your larger funnel each and every time they enter your site, and nurture them towards becoming a valuable customer.

If you are more of a service-based business, then your sales funnel should be to book an appointment with you download an ebook that you have written or are offering, or anything similar that allows a contact or push to an end-action. You will also need to "productise" your service with specific packages in order to make the purchase transaction easier to accomplish.

www.TheDigitalDelusion.com

Every time a visitor touches your website, whether or not they make a purchase, they need to be guided along the way towards your ultimate goal of a sale or some type of contact. This chapter is designed to help you understand what type of sales funnel you need for your business, how best to implement it, and inform you what specific tools are required along the way to really make it work.

This Frame also covers key areas of understanding for developing and building your sales process funnel, to increase your sales. This includes:

- Product development and creating an ascending transaction model for your business with free gifts and other incentives for your audience. You need to offer "Gifts" that move the user towards your core products, as well as workshops, webinars, etc. This will move people along your sales funnel towards your core business.

- Creating and evolving your Key Performance Indicators and metrics for your website and online business, so that you can actually measure your success.

- Webinars & planning. Establish a webinar that is part of your sales funnel, regardless of what your product or service is.

- Subscription and EDM Management. Learning how to use email marketing to reinforce and complement your regular marketing. Make your "news" worth reading.

How Does It Work?

Like most things in life, it is fundamental to ensure that you have goals. Visitors are "captured" and used as best as possible towards your business goals. As in life, if you don't have a clear plan or goal in terms of what you want to accomplish, then you probably won't actually be able to get there.

Online business is no different. Goals need to be set; not just for you and your business in terms of sales, etc. but also towards being able to measure and ascertain whether or not any of your goals are in fact practical and useful to your business.

An online goal is a way of measuring specific activity. Once you establish your online goals and put in place the tools to be able to measure and analyse them, then you can be better informed of what your customer is doing and how they are going about it. This allows you to better target the specific needs of each and every one of your clients.

Every link, status and activity should tie in somehow with the over-riding goal or sales funnels that you are creating and generating for your business.

A goal can be:
- Download an ebook
- Link to a specific page
- Email or call directly
- Make a purchase
- Make a booking
- Send out a tweet from your page
- Specific social actions
- Webinar registration
- Online participation event
- Inquiries
- Leads
- Sales
- Referrals

The purpose of goals are to:
1. Elevate Brand perception
2. Establish thought leadership
3. Drive customer engagement

www.TheDigitalDelusion.com

4. Provide better customer service
5. Increase customer retention
6. Build a larger referral network

What You Need To Do.

1. Establish a method of contact for your audience, such as email list management and auto responders.
2. Outline and detail what your sales funnel is. What is your outcome? What are your goals?
3. Decide how can you use online advertising to grow interest and awareness in your online activities?
4. Identify what you consider to be a "goal". Is it a specific action that you want your customer to do? Once you have identified and created your goals, you can then establish the benchmark by attaching a specific Google Analytics goal.
5. Decide on what webinar services you can use? What topics do you need to address? How do you tie in your webinars with your overall content planning from Frame 2?

What you need to do next

1. Establish your product "gifts".
2. Create your "Product for Prospects", such as webinars, workshops, seminars.
3. Ensure you have your core service created as a product, and as part of a package.
4. Establish your communication channels through email, and auto responders.

Frame #7: Advertising & Analytics
Increase your audience awareness with key advertising, and improve your online activities by analyzing your results

What Is It?

Advanced online strategies include the utilisation of tools and methodologies that allow you to further refine your business activity and ensure that your business is continually evolving online.

The business basics required are in Frames 1-6; these are the primary activities that you must develop and enhance your skills in. Frame 7 is executed when you are ready to truly step up and implement activities and strategies that no one, including your competition, is using effectively. It now allows you to expand your audience base, and implement and manage your new online empire.

By combining core knowledge with these additional strategies, it will allow you to advance your business online. You will build something that has a lot of staying power, creating a higher level of competitiveness. You will ultimately be able to expand your audience base.

Frame 7 consists of the following core activities that will further develop and enhance your business and how you continue to grow and build it:

- Setting "Goals" and measurements with Google Analytics - While these have been established with your website and sales funnel, they also need to evolve further during this stage. These are the measurable goals or activities that need to move people through your sales funnel, but also to be able to measure and identify what is happening.
- Advertising on Facebook, Linkedin, Google, Yahoo and any other advertising networks.

- Analytics & Measurement - Analytics is the combination of data analysis and statistics. In order to be truly effective and understand what is going on, you need to be able to get the information that helps you make business appropriate decisions online.

- Managing Multiple Channels - While it is important to have a focus in all of your online activities, it is also necessary to use a variety of channels to further develop your online influence.

- Toolkit/Dashboard - As your business expands, and you become more engaged online, you will need to ensure that your messaging is unified, and more importantly, cohesive with your overall message. Efficiency is key, as a dashboard allows you to message consistently across multiple channels, simultaneously.

- Coordinating offline and online activities - One of the downfalls of modern business is the fact that there appears to be a firewall between offline and online activities. Your offline messaging must be congruent with your online messaging.

- Reporting - While this ties in with analytics, it is important that you structure information that is valuable to you and your business. What are your KPIs? What are your business objectives? What are you actually able to measure?

- Return on Investment - Now that you have all components working together, you can actually develop and enhance your ROI. Utilising an ROI measurement is now something that will actually work, and actually make sense. The reason that a lot of businesses stay away from ROI is simply that they are scared of what the result may indicate. Once you have all of the pieces in place, then you will readily be able to calculate a proper ROI in all of your online endeavours.

How Does It Work?

These final strategies allow you and your business to further refine your business activities, and become more precise in their execution. Creating congruency between all activities is critical to ensure a sound strategy, however more so it also creates unity with your customers.

These activities also ensure that you are enabling your customers across all of the channels that you operate in, and giving you a competitive advantage.

When you have established a complete and comprehensive platform, only then will you get the most advantage out of advertising, as the base for your advertising platform will be ready. You can then expand your influence outside your online community, outside your initial sphere of influence. Many businesses waste an incredible amount of money because they choose to advertise without having a complete platform. This means they will not be able to move people towards their sales funnel; they are not able to properly capture the leads that they need. When the platform is complete, you can move people to any specific place that you want.

What You Need To Do.

Answer the following questions for your additional understanding:

- How do you measure your online success, in terms of traffic?
- How can you make your online workflow efficient?
- How are you actually measuring and analysing what your customer is doing online with your website and your other online properties? How do these relate to your KPI's?
- What Dashboard and CRM can you use that best fits with your overall goals and the outcomes you want for your website?

What you need to do next.

1. Set up analytics for your website. Analysis what is important to you and your business.

2. Create advertising campaigns that are focused on a very small niche market, in order to create the biggest interest and gains. Test your campaigns. Establish niche landing page through such services to unbounce.com, to further enhance and learn from your marketing and advertsing efforts

3. Organise your social media and blog posts with a dashboard and management tool, such as Hootsuite, Cyfe.

Download all of the Online Empire Project Questionnaires to build and grow your business.

Scan QR Code or Link here: www.thedigitaldelusion.com/1

"Photographs will be telegraphed from any distance. If there be a battle in China a hundred years hence, snapshots of its most striking events will be published in the newspapers an hour later... photographs will reproduce all of the nature's colours."

- John Elfreth Watkins, Engineer, 1900

What You Need To Know

This chapter takes a look at the post-steps and milestones that you need to undertake to get the job done and to become remarkable with your business, online.

You will learn:

1. How to connect the 7-Frame Online Empire Project with your business.
2. How to create a schedule that works for your business implementation.
3. Some tools and activities that you can undertake to help you move forward.

The New Digital Manifesto

> I will take control of my own business online.
> No one knows my business better than myself.
> I refuse to be mislead by the industry.
> I am taking charge of my own business, in my own industry.
> I will concentrate on what is important, and disregard the misinformation that is prevalent.
> I will become the leader in my industry. I will surpass my competitors.
> I will no longer be deluded by what others say and cause me to think.
> I will become the master of my own digital domain.
> I will build my online empire.

Rules of ENGAGEment

There is no time to rest. You now have in your hands the exact tools and methodology that will make a difference in excelling your business. All of the elements, all of the pieces, all of the strategies that work; you have got everything that you need.

We have created the clarity for what you can do for your business, online. We are ready to support you as well, on your new journey towards becoming the leader in your industry. Are you ready to take the plunge?

Make it happen. No excuses. Get shit done.

Now that you have connected all the pieces, here are several things that you need to do:

1. Calculate and utilise ROI. You have an understanding of what your costs are. For those of you who are obsessed with ROI - go calculate it. If you don't care about ROI - don't calculate it. Either way, you will see exactly what you need to do now.

2. Continue into the building stages of your business. The foundation is set, now you need to continue to build your "home". This means that you have to continue to develop your channels and maintain and build your schedule, among other things. Create a master schedule that

www.TheDigitalDelusion.com

you can use to break down your content, and to break down all of the activities that you need to complete.

3. Create a schedule for all of your activities, every 3 months. Three months is an excellent time period to be able to properly gauge what you are doing and see what may or may not be working. It is an opportunity to change things if you feel that they are not working properly.

4. Follow us and join our growing online community. We will have regular updates to our program, new insights into our methodologies, additional checklists and other things to keep the delusions at bay.

Each of the "Frames" will allow you to achieve the goals that you need to complete to get your business exactly where you want it. The important thing is that you need to complete each step consecutively, or at a minimum, concurrently. Each step is designed so that you can build upon the elements that you need, when you need them. It has been maximised to gain the most benefit from each proceeding step.

Keep in mind that this is the foundation for your entire digital domain. It is meant to allow you to set things up and continue to monitor, maintain and manage your entire program. That being said, you will need to continue to keep everything running smoothly with online community management and development.

You can't just set up the entire program and let it out to graze. It won't work that way. You need to be smarter than the rest, and actually manage it regularly. You need to see it grow and build to your online empire. It's not going to get there by itself. Continue to refine your tactics from your overall strategy; continue to put all of the tools that are at your disposal, in place; continue to streamline what you have done, and now what you need to continue to do.

Go through each of these modules several times, and highlight what it is that you need to accomplish for each stage.

Other Resources

There are a number of online resources that are available to further develop and enhance your 7-Frame Online Empire Project. These are broken down into online tools that you can use for the various stages of the Project, as well as specific worksheets and documents that we use for our clients.

Tools

Below are some additional tools that will assist you with further development of your Online Empire Project.

Download new tools from www.thedigitaldelusion.com/1

Link	Online Empire Frame	Item
http://audiojungle.net/	Frame 3: Video	Royalty based sound files for videos
http://www.blogdash.com	Frame 2: Content	Sourcing of blogs
www.toggl.com	Frame 1: Support	Time Tracking
http://basecamp.com/	Frame 1: Support	Project management
http://www.tickspot.com	Frame 1: Support	Time Tracking
https://marketplace.visual.ly/	Frame 4: Video & Visuals	Create infographics for visuals, for your sales funnel
http://www.ereleases.com	Frame 6: Sales Funnel	Press Release services
http://www.agorapulse.com	Frame 7: Advertising & Analytics	Facebook management suite
http://www.clickwebinar.com/features	Frame 6: Webinar Software	Clickwebinar service
http://www.instantpresenter.com	Frame 6: Webinar Software services	Instant Presenter
http://www.pagemodo.com/	Frame 3: Social & Sharing	Facebook Image Creator
http://www.involver.com/	Frame 7: CRM - social media management	
https://www.timetrade.com/td/dashboard.jsp	Frame 6: Sales Funnel	Online Time Booking

URL	Frame	Purpose
http://www.jotform.com/form-templates/	Frame 6: Sales Funnel	Creating forms for online use, surveys, event registration, etc.
http://www.gatective.com/	Frame 7: Analytics	Analytics verification
https://magic.piktochart.com/	Frame 4: Video & Visuals	Create infographics
http://visual.ly	Frame 4: Video & Visuals	Create infographics
http://unbounce.com/	Frame 6: Sales funnel	Create landing pages
http://www.instapage.com	Frame 6: Sales funnel	Create landing pages

Online Empire Project - Resources

Download the following kits:

1. Strategy Planning Questionnaire
2. Sample Strategic Architecture
3. Content Planning Questionnaire
4. Website specification
5. Blog Template
6. Social & Sharing Outlines
7. Other worksheets

Free downloads and additional tools and resources available at www.thedigitaldelusion.com/1

Create A Master Schedule

The Digital Delusion Online Empire Project is a finite program. The 7 Frames are designed like modules and checkpoints to keep you on track.

Create a giant master schedule or table that lists all milestones, and approximate details of each, along with the timings (weekly, daily, monthly, etc.). For simplicity, start with a 3-month schedule, that will allow you to begin the steps to create consistency across all channels.

Your schedule needs to include:
- Auto responders
- EDM
- Video posts
- Photo posts
- Blog posts
- Gifts, downloads
- Webinars, workshops
- Social posting
- Videos
- Visuals
- Gifts
- Advertising
- Personas
- Themes
- website
- events
- landing pages

When you are building your schedule, consider what channels you will be using, as well as how you will be delivering your message. Build some consistency as well; produce content that is regular, focussed and appeals to your specific personas of your core audience.

Address these issues:

1. Channel(s) of distribution
2. Type of content
3. Relation and context of content
4. Timing of content (day, month, week)
5. Persona that you are speaking to
6. Themes and topics that you can develop
7. Frequency of posts/content

And of course, don't forget who is responsible, as well as measuring your results.

Your New Scorecard

Now that everything is in order, we need to take a look at where things are for you; what your new baseline is, and will continue to be.

Consider the following 6 Criteria:

1. Search Engine Ranking
2. Keyword Effectiveness
3. Social Media Affinity
4. Online Visibility
5. Content Structure
6. Strategic Architecture

Do you recall the three strategy elements discussed at the beginning? Take a look in terms of your business development from the standpoint of Strategy, Knowledge, and Awareness & Relevance. On a scale of 1 to 10, how do you score your business?

Fill in your scores here:

1. Strategy: _____

2. Knowledge: _____

3. Awareness & Relevance: _____

Now, ask yourself, how has it improved?

Complete an online assessment of where you and your business currently sit. Find out what your Online Empire Score is.

Complete a scorecard every 3 months to ensure that you remain on track.

Your Free Entrepreneur Online Training Course

Want to take your understanding to the next level, to further build your digital platform? As a reader of this book, you are entitled to receive my free training program, which includes dozens of key downloads, over 20 hours of videos and complete instructions to build your complete digital platform and grow your successful business online.

To receive full details on how to register for your free Entrepreneurs Online Training Course, simply send an email to:

thebook@thedigitaldelusion.com

Education

Education is important in everything that we do. We need to teach everyone the principles that have been laid out, so that everyone can learn from them, and take the industry back from the brink.

Education and training has been a central focus throughout my life, and I value the ability to teach others. I have spent many years teaching and mentoring entrepreneurs, students, and people who are just interested in the exciting world of business. I've taught young students who didn't really know what business was about, to people who have decided to take on a new career challenge.

How does education fit in with the Digital Delusion?

There is a tremendous amount of misinformation and misguidance out there. How do we stop this or simply reduce it?

1. Learn about your own business.
2. Understand how the pieces fit together. Educate yourself about what is important - only you can be the expert.
3. Invest the time, energy and resources needed to establish yourself and your activities.
4. Question who gives you advice and why they are doing it.
5. Educate others. Let them know what the digital delusions are, and more importantly, how to overcome them by systematic, simple solutions. Consider establishing delusion debates with your business peers to isolate other problems that are present. Consider teaching others just getting into business, what they need to be aware of. Help them avoid making the same mistakes as you have in the past.

The only way to eliminate the delusions is to understand them. The only way to understand them is to learn about them. The only way to learn about them is to educate others. Tell others how they can overcome these digital delusions.

Want to contribute to the education side of the Digital Delusion to ensure that we can all start to learn what we really need to know?

Go to www.thedigitaldelusion.com/1 to connect with some of these additional resources:

- Download the complete ebook for free
- Find out if we are speaking in your area
- Put on a seminar or workshop in your city or area
- Join Our Team
- Join an introductory webinar
- Find a workshop in your area
- Ask me a question! Call +61413106880; email education@thedigitaldelusion.com

Need to purchase bulk editions of The Digital Delusion and other educational materials at an educational discounted price? Please contact us at education@thedigitaldelusion.com

"There is no reason anyone would want a personal computer in their home."
— Ken Olson,
Digital Equipment founder, 1977

Delusional?

Discover all of the tools and planning activities that will further enhance your digital platform.
Scan QR Code or Link here: www.thedigitaldelusion.com/1

Where to find us! Join the conversation!

The digital delusion is everywhere!

Find us (and me, the author), here:

www.about.me/doylebuehler

www.facebook.com/doyle.buehler

www.facebook.com/thedigitaldelusion

au.linkedin.com/in/doylebuehler/

http://instagram.com/doylebuehler

Discover more links:

www.thedigitaldelusion.com/1

Want to send an "old-fashioned" email? Please email me:

doyle@thedigitaldelusion.com

OTHER PRODUCTS & SERVICES

What is The Digital Delusion?

The Digital Delusion is more than just a book and a way of creating business. It is an "anti" Agency. It is a way of doing business. It is a new way of thinking and implementing for businesses wanting to become Leaders in their industry.

We are creating a new awareness and understanding of what is needed to succeed online. It is about mastering the digital domain and creating clarity and confidence online for your business.

It is about helping entrepreneurs and business leaders cut through the clutter and confusion of being online, so that they can become remarkable.

There has never been a better time to take control of your business, and become the online business leader that you are.

We leave entrepreneurs feeling awesome, online.

Please go to www.thedigitaldelusion.com to continue to stay informed and stay involved, and find out what works for your business:

- Email sign-up list
- Videos
- Scheduled Webinars
- Scheduled Workshops
- Digital Delusion Gifts

Want to grow your business further? Ask us about Licensing, Franchising and coaching services.

We have come a long way. We started out understanding the industry as one big delusion. Now we are more in tune with what we are supposed to be doing.

It's still not going to be easy; but it is going to be much clearer for you. Comprehension and knowledge is key.

The journey doesn't stop here either; you need to keep going. Develop your online empire. Make your project work like it should. Become the entrepreneur that you know you are.

We've seen it before. Remember when someone exposes to the world how magicians and/or illusionists trick people, all of the other magicians or illusionists get mad at him for spilling the beans? We've given you the "reveal" moment. Now you have that "a-ha" feeling, and subsequently you will get a much clearer understanding of what you have just accomplished.

Well, we are about to spill the beans and ruin it for all of those ad agencies, SEO, PPC and online "support" companies trying to trick you into buying their services. The ones that are keeping you fooled into paying them; the ones that keep you delusional in running your business online...

You now know what to look for and what to look out for, as you become a truly remarkable entrepreneur.

"It's not magic. It's business."

Take what you have learned, and use it. Manage it and make it better. Change what you are doing and improve what you can do.

ACKNOWLEDGMENTS

Special thanks to:

Andrew Griffiths, a wonderful mentor and best-selling author, who has guided my entire process. A true inspiration.

Daniel Priestly, Glen Carlson, and everyone at the Key Person of Influence Program who have helped me unleash and focus my entrepreneur strengths.

CROWDFUNDING & SUPPORTERS

One of the most exciting things about the digital age, is the ability to create a community around the world. The newest way to leverage this is through crowdfunding; the ability to gather financial supporters from around the world.

I chose to create a crowdfunding campaign in order to leverage the costs of funding and creating a book. In the process, I've created a new, supportive community from around the world who are interested in the entrepreneur revolution, from where ever they are. It was also created as a new insight into new digital development. Crowdfunding will become a bigger and bigger player to all entrepreneurs.

Here is a link to the original crowdfunding campaign; you can continue to contribute to the page, as well as for additional rewards. We were successful in raising over $5000 for the support of the first run of the book.

www.pozible.com/thedigitaldelusion

There were a number of "Rewards" offered, when a pledge was provided. This included starting with simple "Armchair Entrepreneurs", up to consulting services.

I want to thank all of the contributors for their support. It has been an amazing experience and opportunity.

Doyle Buehler

Thank you to all of the Crowdfunding Campaign Supporters

The New Book on Digital Innovation and Entrepreneurship

Pledge Now + Rewards

Overcoming the Clutter and Confusion of Online Digital Strategy and Social Media

A$5,769 Pledged of A$5,625 Target

0 Mins to go
Deadline 18th June 2013 at 12:00 pm EST

58 Supporters

Olga Fischer   Dave McGill   Eduardo Gomes
Cheryl Ng   Geoff Hetherington   Javier Schwersensky
Dave Walker   Pei-Shan Wu   Rex Wood   Wanda Nyirfa
Elly Sumich   Robert Bihar   Andrew O'Connell
    Cimone-Louise Fung   Rob Walker
Lawrence & Adele Buehler   Emma Lundwall
Amanda Fisher   Andrew Griffiths   Carla Castro
Skeeve Stevens   Charlie Grzyb
David J Peach   Alanna Quigley   Michelle Astudillo
Tina Newhook   Anneka Manning   Steve beal
    Duncan Isaksen-Loxton   Jane Holliday   Kris Pokler
Geoff Anderson   Carole Marshall   Darren Fast
    Ariel lazaro   Amy Luscombe   Thomas Kelshaw   K Buehler
Ronnie Kagan   Lori Sumich   Gina Lednyak
Lyle Greig   Kathleen Chai Latte   Gina Lednyak
Naveen Somia   Nick Edwards   Jasper Vallance
Tracey Baxter   Karina Grant   Jack Peterson
    Manuela Vianna
Justine Armstrong   Larisa Ishchenko
Lori Sumich   Zanna Joyce

www.thedigitaldelusion.com/1

Thank you to all of the Crowdfunding Supporters! You Rock!

REFERENCES

Priestley, D. (2011). Become a Key Person of Influence. Hertfordshire, UK: Ecademy Press.

Niels Bosma, Sander Wennekers and José Ernesto Amorós. The Global Entrepreneurship Monitor (GEM) 2011 Global Report.

Roberts, Kevin (2005). Lovemarks: The Future Beyond Brands (Expanded edition ed.). New York, NY: PowerHouse Books.

Degrees of Separation in Social Networks
    Reza Bakhshandeh, Mehdi Samadi, Zohreh Azimifar, Jonathan Schaeffer
    Retrieved from http://www.aaai.org/ocs/index.php/OCS/SOCS11/paper/view/4031

Google, Zero Moment of Truth Research Paper
    Retrieved from: http://www.google.com.au/think/collections/zero-moment-truth.html

State of Mobile 2013 Infographic, Supermonitoring.com, retrieved from: http://www.supermonitoring.com/blog/2013/09/23/state-of-mobile- 2013-infographic/

BIBLIOGRAPHY

Velosa, Maria. Web Copy That Sells. American Management Association. NY 2013

Nahai, Nathalie. Webs of Influence: The Psychology of Online Persuasion. Pearson, Sydney 2012

Handley, A., Chapman, C.C. Content Rules. John Wiley & Sons, NY 2013

DOWNLOAD THE FREE PDF VERSION OF THE DIGITAL DELUSION

Get a digital PDF copy for your smartphone, tablet or ebook reader. Email doyle@thedigitaldelusion.com to get your free copy now.

ABOUT THE AUTHOR

Doyle Buehler is a writer, entrepreneur, speaker and professional business strategy and marketing consultant. From several successful start-ups and retail franchise businesses in Canada and the United States, to helping other companies succeed with their ideas and strategies, he has spent over 10 years in the business world making things happen – both online and off. During his previous business development, he grew a multi-million dollar online ecommerce company around the world from Canada, expanding extensively into the United States, Europe and then Australia.

He is a Leading innovator in the online, ecommerce world. He has helped businesses grow and achieve their goals through harnessing their knowledge, expertise and entrepreneurial spirit. He has also presented and keynoted at numerous marketing and technology seminars in Canada and the United States.

Major work projects include ecommerce, web development, Search Engine Optimisation, Social Media Marketing, Social Media Training, Search Engine Marketing, and online Advertising.

Currently, as a digital strategy and online marketing professional consultant, he is creating exciting and compelling digital-focused marketing strategies and implements them with quality, consistency and professionalism.

He teaches insights into digital marketing, including training in social media, as well as entrepreneurship and business planning. He writes for a number of blogs on business, strategy, online marketing, web business, digital media, social media, trends and subjects of interest to all entrepreneurs.

Doyle was nominated for the Ernest C. Manning Innovation award for software and operational systems that he managed and developed for his start-up businesses. He is the holder of two international patents for consumer products and online technology customisation methods.

He was awarded his Masters of Business in 2002 for his Thesis on "Mass Customisation in the Retail Consumer Environment", from Royal Roads University, in Victoria, Canada. This was the beginning of the entrepreneur adventure for Doyle, as it formed the basis of the subsequent business start-ups in the ensuing years.

One of the online businesses that he started and led, mytego.com, was named as "Profit Magazine's Hot 50 Fastest Growing Companies in Canada" in 2008, as well as the "Manitoba Business Magazine's #1 Fastest Growing Company" for the State, in 2009.

The digital framework that was developed for this book was also awarded the 2013 "Smart 100" Award for Innovation from Australian Anthill Magazine.

Doyle has always been actively involved in the business community, providing mentorship for new entrepreneurs for the Canadian Youth Business Foundation Program, Junior Achievement, as well as other collegiate entrepreneurship programs. He has also served on many Council and Entrepreneur Boards, as well as creating several distinctive Entrepreneur Business Networking organizations.

His online experience has been utilised in various global industries, including travel, fashion insurance, pharmaceuticals, banking, investment, hospitality, financial, events and learning domains.

www.ingramcontent.com/pod-product-compliance
Ingram Content Group UK Ltd.
Pitfield, Milton Keynes, MK11 3LW, UK
UKHW041429180426
11947UKWH00007B/359